QUICKEST WAY TO EVERYTHING GOOD

YOU CAN GET WHAT YOU WANT IF YOU PUT THIS FIRST

DR. ROBERT A. RUSSELL

Audio Enlightenment Press

Giving Voice to the Wisdom of the Ages

Printed in the United States of America

First Printing, 2022
ISBN 978-1-941489-87-1

www.RobertARussell.Org

Note To The Student

This book is one of a series of four consecutive metaphysical studies on the Parable of the Prodigal Son and the Elder Brother. The books are listed in the order in which they should be read.

1. YOU CAN GET WHAT YOU WANT IF YOU FIND IT WITHIN YOURSELF.

2. VITAL POINTS IN DEMONSTRATION.
    You Can Get What You Want
    If You Return Home.

3. THE QUICKEST WAY TO EVERYTHING GOOD.
    You Can Get What You Want
    If You Put This First.

4. TALK YOURSELF INTO IT.
    You Can Get What You Want
    If You Talk Yourself Into It.

Table of Contents

The Key .... **x**

I   The Quick Response 1

      Streamlining Your Prayers 7

      Releasing the Kingdom of God 22

      Capitulation 26

II   Awakening the Power 29

      Is It the Eleventh Hour in Your Case? 32

      Big Difficulties Are Your Big Moments 34

      The Unchanging Power 36

      Awakening the Power 37

      Don't Outline 45

      Do Not Hold On To the Old 46

      Do Not Contract the Power 47

      Helping God Help Us 52

      Practice the Presence of God 55

      Place All Your Affairs Lovingly
      in God's Hands 55

      Depend Upon the Christ Within You For All Things
      At All Times 57

      Change Your Mind and You Will
      Change Your Life 57

      Act Always With God 58

      Be Positive to Your Good 60

III   "God Is . . . A Very Present Help in Trouble" 62

How to Think of Trouble 63

The Poised Mind 66

Harnessing the Emotions 68

Your Biggest Problem 71

Get An Ideal 72

Give Up Self-Management 74

"Transformed Into the Same Image" 76

The Involuntary Principle of Living 78

Give God First Place 79

Get a Sense of Dominion 81

IV   "Thy Kingdom Come" in My Problems 84

The Problem of Sickness 86

Right Work 86

The Disagreeable Person 88

Faultfinding and Criticism 88

The Grudge Carrier 89

Fear of Inherited Traits 91

Inferiority 92

Doubt 96

Discouragement 101

A Parable 105

V   Big Difficulties and Little Difficulties 108

"Thy Kingdom Come On Earth As It Is in Heaven" 126

Thinking and Working in The Absolute 132

Failure Is a Teacher 139

The Human Tendency 141

Confession 143

Put the Kingdom of God First 145

Is This True in Your Case? 147

According to Your Faith 149

Bless Your Circumstances 151

Cooperating With the Kingdom 152

You Cannot Change God 156

LIFE AS IT IS, AND AS PLANNED BY GOD . . .

HEALTH, SUCCESS, JOY, HAPPINESS, STRENGTH, DOMINION, WEALTH, FAITH, CONFIDENCE, CERTAINTY, PEACE, POWER, PLENTY, POISE, COURAGE, LOVE, HARMONY, FREEDOM

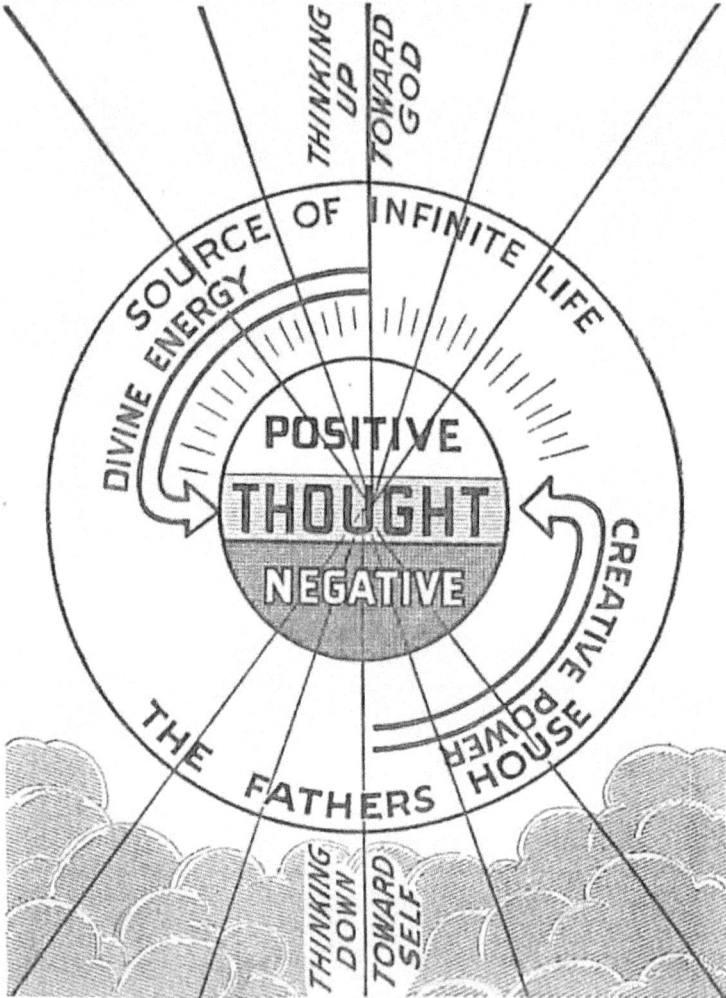

DISEASE, FAILURE, SORROW, MISERY, WEAKNESS, INFERIORITY, POVERTY, UNHAPPINESS, WORRY, FEAR, DOUBT, LOSS, TROUBLE, LIMITATIONS, DISCORD, PROBLEMS, BONDAGE

LIFE AS WE MAKE IT BY OUR NEGATIVE THINKING

Explanation Of Diagram

If you will study the diagram on the opposite page, you will see that the power flowing from God through man is neither good nor bad as the human mind usually understands it. It is simply Divine Energy — Creative Power. The energy that is turned into failure, sickness and discord and other negative expressions in no way differs from the energy that manifests in success, health, peace and other forms of good. The difference is not in the energy, or Creative Power, but in the thought that turns it either into constructive channels or destructive channels.

How important it is, then, that we keep our thoughts centered in the constructive and affirmative side of Good and guarded against the destructive side of evil, so that only the good can manifest in our lives — the riches of life instead of its limitations.

The Key

If the things you do not care for come to you easily, then the way to get the things that you do care for is to make them of no importance and of no value in your thought. Jesus gave us the Law governing this principle of demonstration in His statement about the seed. "Except a grain of wheat fall into the earth and die, it abideth alone (has no power); but if it die, it beareth much fruit."

The seed, of course, is the desire; the ground is the creative medium of the subconscious mind, and the dropping of the seed into the earth is symbolical of the releasing of the desire from the conscious thought so that the Law can work freely for its fulfillment.

Just as seed kept in a package will not grow and bring forth its increase, so a desire held tightly in the personal thought cannot be fulfilled. Jesus said: "See it in instant fulfillment. Give thanks." Forget it by taking all thought, anxiety, worry, concern, fear, value or importance from it. Give it up. Let it go. Release the consciousness back of the desire, and the result is assured. Thus, the quickest way to demonstrate your desires is to adopt "an attitude of happy indifference" toward them.

THE QUICKEST WAY TO EVERYTHING GOOD

You Can Get What You Want If You Put This First

I
The Quick Response

"Seek ye first the Kingdom of God, and His righteousness; and all these things shall be added unto you." Matt. 6:33.

This book is unusual in that it gives you a short-cut to answered prayer and a quick way to God. It not only tells you the quickest way to everything good, but the shortest way out of everything evil. There are, of course, those who will assure you that there are no short cuts in spiritual work and no quick ways to spiritual manifestation, but Jesus told us plainly that there are. So, we declare that this book is unusual because it gives you this wonderful revelation.

All Truth students believe in eventual demonstration but few have faith in instant manifestation. Immediate answers, in our present state of consciousness, are more the exception than the rule. They are regarded more in the light of miracles than the orderly outworking of spiritual law. It is our purpose, therefore, to show the reverse of this order, and to prove that instant demonstrations should be commonplace.

Since immediate manifestations do occur, as every healer and minister will tell you, then there is no reason why they should not be frequent. Touching this subject, Jesus said: "The Kingdom of Heaven [source of all good] is at hand." "The fields . . . are white already to harvest." "Before they call, I will answer; and while they are yet speaking, I will hear."

Then, why do we fail to demonstrate more rapidly; why are our answers delayed? Because we still believe more in

1

the kingdom of this world than in the Kingdom of God. We have not only divided our minds between the lower and the Higher, but we have divided them unevenly. We still are about ninety percent with John Doe and only ten percent with God. In other words, the preponderance of our power and faith is still centered in the human mind with its false beliefs and delays.

No one will deny that delay is of the human mind, and that it is unknown to the Christ Mind. "The Kingdom of Heaven is at hand." God is NOW. The Law of the Spirit is perfect, instant, omni-active and automatic. The Law always works in the present, and "is compelled by its very nature to return to the thinker exactly what he thinks into it."

Then why so many delayed answers! Because of the greater activity of human beliefs. We neutralize our good by the acceptance of thoughts of limitation and delay. We assert that "The Word of God is instant and powerful and that it always works." But this is true only when we shift the center of power from the human to the Christ mind, and KEEP our thinking in accord with Spirit.

That is what St. Paul meant when he said, "Seek those things which are above, where Christ is." Seek a more perfect alignment with God's Law of Good. When instant healings and demonstrations are made, it is because we have, consciously or unconsciously, turned aside all human beliefs of limitation and accepted our good as instantly here.

The two which "God hath joined together, and no man shall put asunder" are the Christ Mind and the human mind. "Of mine own self [without Christ—by the human mind alone]," said Jesus, "I can do nothing." Why not? Because our thinking must be in absolute accord with Spirit before an instant manifestation can take place.

That is the requirement of God's quick response, and anyone not complying with it may expect delays and disappointments in his progress. The human mind is the repository of uncertainty and unfulfilled desires. It is powerful only when it is detached from self and when it is thinking with God.

Let us not forget, as St. Paul said, that Spiritual things are spiritually discerned. Spirit manifests through Spirit and not through human thoughts. "Like begets like." Each mind pays in its own coin. If we pray with the human mind, the result is disappointment and delay. If we pray with the Christ Mind, then we get spiritual results—"all things whatsoever we desire," in instant fulfillment.

Spiritual promises are guaranteed in the present and nowhere else. "NOW is the accepted time." "Now is the day of salvation." Now is the day of freedom, release, revelation, healing and fulfillment. God is omnipresent, omnipotent and omniscient. Spirit is everywhere equally present. The Kingdom of Heaven is finished. God's perfect work is now in manifestation. Your prayer is answered. Your desires are fulfilled. Your problem is solved. Your needs are met. Your body is healed. The thing you seek is already here.

But now we are face to face with the greatest problem of all—the great chasm between Dives and Lazarus, between prayer and answer, between desire and fulfillment. "And beside all this, between us and you there is a great gulf fixed: so that they who would pass from hence to you cannot; neither can they pass to us, that would come from thence."

"The great gulf that is fixed between Dives and Lazarus is the great gulf that is fixed between all people and their good who try to approach it with a divided mind. Then how shall we bridge this gulf? How shall we bring these truths into objective manifestation? Shall we do it by trying to introduce a fourth dimensional consciousness into a mind that has only a three-dimensional capacity? Shall we do it by trying to live in self and God at one and the same time? No. It cannot be done in any of these ways."

Jesus said you must die to self before you can live in God. You must leave one plane of consciousness before you can live in another. You must "lose your life to find it." You must renounce the little self before the larger Self can be realized. You must surrender the relative before you can enter the Absolute. You must let go of the old before you can take hold of the new. You must be a voice instead of an echo. You must think with your Christ mind and stop reacting with your emotions.

Does all this sound vague and mysterious? Then stop reading further until you understand every sentence in the paragraph above, until you have thoroughly mastered and understood what each means. This has to do with the establishment of the Kingdom of God in your life, which is the quickest way to everything good.

St. Paul said: "Let this Mind be in you, which was also in Christ Jesus." You have heard and read that statement many times, but maybe you have never understood what it means. It means that "the degree to which we allow the Christ Mind to work through us will determine the degree to which we manifest God in our affairs.

"The more we exclude the human thought, and the idea of the power of human thought and align our human mind with the Christ Mind in recognizing God as the only Power and the only Cause, the greater will be our desire to behold God instantly in His perfect manifestation. When we think in unity with Spirit our desires are fulfilled.

"Any one who desires instant results should speak the word for them. The more we subordinate human thought and comprehend the spiritual realization, the sooner will our treatments bring instant results."

There are five steps in instant manifestation and the sooner we master them the sooner we shall get quick responses in our work. They are these:

(1) **To subordinate all human thoughts and beliefs and to think wholly with the Spirit — in conscious unity with God.**
(2) **To recognize the Good as instantly here.**
(3) **To accept the idea of immediacy in our consciousness.**
(4) **To recognize that "there is no distance, no change, no time, no space In Omnipresence."**
(5) **To accept the Kingdom of God as a present Reality.**

These five steps are vitally important and it will pay you to meditate upon them (involve them in your mind) until they become active in your consciousness: "When you are ready, I will do the works through you." Know this. Realize it. Contemplate it. Embody it. Then immediacy will begin to develop in your demonstrations. Demonstrations will come not because you have changed God, or have tried to "make" Him do your bidding, but because you are no longer · qualifying your acceptance of Good by a human (contrary) belief in evil.

"Not everyone who saith unto me, Lord, Lord, shall enter the Kingdom of Heaven; but he that doeth the will of my Father who is in heaven." The Source of Infinite Good is contacted and is released to us: not by hoping, wishful thinking, or mental gymnastics, but by a changed consciousness—the "pure in heart," the new born, the one-pointed, the Christ-Minded, the God-Centered, the self-surrendered and the Kingdom-possessed.

Most people think of the Will of God as some inscrutable purpose in the Universe that is contrary to their own. They think of It as a passive resignation to defeat that which cannot be helped, that which cannot be cured—the unfinished task, the unanswered prayer, the unassuaged grief the unfulfilled desire.

To Jesus, the will of God meant not only the right use of the individual will, but, being inside God's Intention, the perfect pattern for man, the ultimate realization of the Divine Goal, the final security against an outrageous world. It meant the sense of freedom from responsibility, either for things past or things future, the final dissolution of conflicts and evil. It meant that nothing could ever defeat God or the mind that was centered in Him.

"Thy will be done" means literally this: Let God have His Perfect Way in me and in all my affairs. God, being the Originator and Source of all Good, cannot will anything but Goodness. Thus the will that is surrendered to Him cannot initiate or attract to itself anything but Good. It is, at the same time, both man's power to accomplish things and God 's power to change that which needs to be changed.

We must be careful, however, never to use our will for anything but constructive purposes. The will is never creative but always directive. We do not use it for compelling or willing things to happen, but to provide ways for them to happen. Jesus said: "Which of you, by taking thought, can add one cubit to his stature?" It is obvious from this that any other use of the will is destructive. Its only purpose is to "hold the line" While setting new interior forces in action.

They not only must be able to say "I will," but "I can." Strengthen your will, then, if need be but only for the purpose of helping you to think, feel and act with God. Remove the vagueness and uncertainty from your mind, and there will be no limit to what you can do.

STREAMLINING YOUR PRAYERS

This is an age of streamlining. The old is giving way to the new. Everywhere unnecessary impediments and surfaces are being removed. Anything that would offer resistance to our ongoing must be eliminated. We need streamlining not only for our trains, automobiles and airplanes, but in our government, in our homes, business, education, conversation, personal habits and religion.

"Parish house paralysis" now must give way to the cultivation of the consciousness of the Presence of God. Church suppers and parties now must be supplemented by refreshments for the mind and soul. We need to learn how to "Be still and know" that He is God; to have faith in Him as the Source of all our Good.

We need to learn how to make ourselves magnets for that which we desire; to learn how to expand our consciousness until it includes every good thing — not in some future time or place, but NOW. We need to learn how to speak the Word for instant results, how to neutralize the contrary thoughts and beliefs which only deny our word and delay our good.

We hear much in the metaphysical field these days about the space between the prayer and the answer, but very few of us take the trouble to find out what it means. The space here referred to is the time element in realization and it is determined entirely by one's proximity to God's Presence. In the truest sense, there is no more delay between the prayer and the answer than the length of time it takes to turn on the electric light in a darkened room.

"Before they call, I will answer; and while they are yet speaking, I will hear." In other words the light is already on. The good you are seeking is already in manifestation.

Now ask yourself if there could be anything quicker than the Divine Response, anything quicker than "before you call." Then where does the space or postponement enter into prayer? It is your failure to see that the Kingdom of God is NOW HERE. Yes, my friend, that is the only reason for delays and the only reason why you ever suffer from the lack of good things. Because you do not believe, do not know, that the Kingdom of God is NOW HERE — that It is in you and that you are in It; and that It responds to you as you make your demands, in faith, upon It.

"On a Princeton college fireplace, this motto is written: 'God is a Scientist not a magician.' The words are those of Professor Einstein.

"Men have always felt that- God was cooperating with them when they cooperated with Him. To the farmer, God was the Great Farmer; because if you obeyed His rules, He did not play tricks on you; He seemed to want your wheat and produce to grow the way His forests grow. So the legal mind has called Him Judge; the builder has called Him Creator; to the student He is the Teacher; to the sportsman the Great Referee; to the biologist the Orderer of Life; to the doctor the Great Physician.

"And the scientist finds that if he works according to His pattern of ideals and of Truth, the Universe works with him. If a mixture of two chemicals in a test tube turns pink or yellow or smells of smoke on Mon-there is a discoverable reason why not. If not there is a discoverable reason why not. If I sow squash, I reap squash. If I pray in the consciousness of a present and finished Kingdom, then I get an immediate answer to prayer. I take out of it exactly what I put into it."

It is obvious, then, that the whole problem of the space between the prayer and the answer can be resolved into two things: realization and cooperation. A doctor says to a patient: "Here is a cure for your ailment. Take it strictly according to instructions, and give it a chance by taking the food and drink, the exercise and rest I prescribe." But if the patient disobeys, fails to cooperate, who but himself is to blame?

If Jesus says to one in trouble, or in need: "Seek ye first the Kingdom of God, and His righteousness; and all these things shall be added unto you," and there is failure to cooperate, who is to blame if his prayer is not answered? Jesus said that He could do no mighty works in Nazareth because the people would not cooperate with Him. He might say the same thing of the people of any place today.

One hears declarations that Christianity has failed, but the fact is it has never been tried. We have not honestly met the requirements.

Jesus said: "Ye shall know (cooperate with) the Truth, and the Truth shall make you free." The Truth, like any other spiritual attribute depends for its success upon cooperation. It is, by its very nature transforming, cleansing, healing, renewing, but it operates (becomes active) only through the mind (knowledge). It will free you, not by persuasion or compulsion, but by the quiet, positive recognition and realization of its presence.

Jesus said you must know it. In other words, it must be a thing of consciousness. You must have knowledge of it. You must have awareness. Truth known with the whole mind is instantly demonstrated.

It is "not by might, nor by power;" not by our much talking in the market place, that the Kingdom comes. Its method is the gentler one of conversion (change of thought) by spiritual truth and an unassailable faith in the Omnipresence and Omnipotence of God. It is never God Who fails, but we who fail to meet the demands of our faith.

The Law is exact, immutable, inexorable. Christ is the same yesterday, today, forever. If God has healed one person of cancer, He can heal all persons of cancer. If He has redeemed one sinner, He can redeem all sinners. If He has saved one victim of alcohol, He can save all such victims. If He has protected one soul in danger. He can protect all souls. If He has saved one business from failure, He can save all businesses from failure. If He has solved one problem, He can solve all problems. The potentiality of one is the possibility of all.

Remember that and act upon it. There can be no exceptions to God's rule that "He maketh His sun to rise on the evil and on the good, and sendeth rain on the just and on the unjust." The promise is that, "All things whatsoever ye desire, when ye pray, believe that ye receive them, and ye shall have them."

Now, let us pause for a moment to consider some particular difficulties and to ask some direct questions. If the author were talking to you in person, he probably would ask some such questions as these: Are you troubled about something? Are you beset with fear and worry? Are you afraid that you are going to fail? Afraid that you will be unable to meet your obligations? Afraid that you win not measure up to your job? Do you feel frustrated and confused, not knowing which way to turn or what to do?

Jesus said: "Seek ye first the Kingdom of God." Put this first and the way WILL be pointed out.

Have you had a misunderstanding with some friend? Is there friction in the home? Are there unpleasant conditions in your office? Are you suffering from slanderous innuendo or worse? Is your hurt so deep and your confusion so great that you do not know how to proceed?

Jesus said: "Seek ye first the Kingdom of God." Put this first and the crooked ways shall be made straight.

Are you sick and in pain? Are you tormented by increasing symptoms? Have material means failed to relieve you? Has the doctor, perhaps, pronounced your case hopeless? Are you frightened almost into insensibility, and grasping for straws?

Jesus said: "Seek ye first the Kingdom of God." Put this first and my God shall supply all your needs.

Are you grief-stricken by the loss of a loved one? Are you so crushed that you cannot eat; so depressed that you feel you do not want to live; so broken-hearted you do not want to go on? Have all the efforts of your friends to help you been unavailing? Does nothing that your loved ones say or do assuage your grief?

Jesus said: "Seek ye first the Kingdom of God." Put this first and the Comforter will come.

Are you in the dark about some vital action? Does everything hinge upon the right outcome? Is the decision you seek so important that all would be ruined if you made a mistake? Is every door closed; has every source failed and does there seem no way out?

Jesus said: "Seek ye first the Kingdom of God." Put this first and the answer will come.

Have you some momentous task to perform, some important duty to discharge, and are not sure you have the ability to handle it? Are you timid and fearful; has your faith slumped and your confidence been so shattered that you lack the courage to go on?

Jesus said: "Seek ye first the Kingdom of God." Center yourself in God. Then when you think God will think through you; when you speak He will speak for you; when you act He will act with you. Put first things first and secondary things will take care of themselves. Then all will come out right. "All these things shall be added unto you." Yes, then everything pertaining to your physical, mental, material and spiritual needs will be met.

Center yourself in God, says Jesus, and you will automatically attract from the Universe everything that you need. It is a guarantee. Meet the requirements ("Seek ye first the

Kingdom of God"), and the result is "all these things." They SHALL be added.

In the opening paragraph of this book, we made a promise that is now going to be fulfilled:

The quickest way to everything good and the shortest way out of everything evil is to "Seek first the Kingdom of God."

That was not just a beautiful idea which Jesus announced to a curious crowd, but a principle in Truth for all time. By it all spiritual demonstrations are made. When you "seek first the Kingdom of God," then you are always on the right side of the Law and in the proper state of mind to receive. Then God is with you and the Universe is back of you, working for you, with you and through you. All things work together for your good.

When you try to reverse this process, however, by seeking things first, then everything is arrayed against you — all things work together for ill and everything turns out wrong.

One reason why it is so hard to live by the Truth in a confused world like ours is that we have become accustomed to evil. When Jesus healed the demoniac and the man became "clothed in his right mind," the scripture says that "the people were afraid." Afraid of what? They were afraid of right-mindedness. We have become so used to crooked thinking that we are afraid of straight thinking; so accustomed to bondage that we actually fear freedom. We are living out of our element and so nothing turns out right.

The NEW YORKER tells of an interesting experiment which bears on this situation. "A pike and a minnow were placed in the same tank, but separated from each other by a plate glass partition. The pike time after time tried to get the minnow and each time received a severe blow from impact with the glass. Finally, after the pike had fully concluded that it was of no use, the glass partition was removed and the minnow swam all about the pike without the pike making any effort to get it.

"The implications · are obvious . . . the pike was limited by his own concepts, and even though the food (the minnow) was placed within his reach, he had not the ability to conceive that it was for him."

The experiment aptly illustrates the divided mind, which is the reason we do not realize more health, peace, supply, happiness and contentment. We have become so accustomed to our partitions that we never find the door. We become so hypnotized by the apparent that we never find the Real. We become so crystallized in the limited that we never find the Unlimited.

Jesus said: Silence the old habits of belief. Part with the old concepts of limitation and defeat. Separate yourself from them. Cut them off. Strangle them. Let them die. "Judge not according to appearances, but judge righteous judgment." Plainly, see life in its true light. Look upon it as a whole.

The growth of a tree is determined by the amount of sun, air and moisture it is able to draw into itself. The growth of a man is determined by the number of false beliefs and erroneous concepts he is able to expunge (drop) from his consciousness. A tree grows by the attraction of outside forces. A consciousness grows by the expulsion of inner enemies.

You may pray and agonize from now till doomsday, but what is in the consciousness will come out in the body and in your affairs. Jesus did not ask that anything be added to Him from the outside world, but only that He might uncover (experience again) the glory that He had with God before the world (human mind) was.

The whole secret of quick and successful demonstration is, therefore, one's ability to separate himself (withdraw his attention) from the undesirable and keep himself (center his mind) in the kingdom of the desirable. The prodigal son tried to do this by running away. He tried to change conditions without changing himself and it could not be done. Centered in self, he lost his friends, and there was no one to help him. He found what every other self-centered person has always found: namely, that what is in the seed will always come out in the plant.

The right way, according to Jesus, is not to move from one location to another, from one set of circumstances to another, but to change our position in the law — to change our attitude toward God. "Look unto me, and be ye saved, all ye ends of the earth." This is the law of plenty and freedom; for we are as rich or as poor, as healthy or as sick, as successful or as limited as the beliefs which we allow to occupy our minds.

We are not separated from our blessings by persons, places, times, conditions or things, but by our limited vision and our inability to see. "The land that thou seest, that will I give unto thee." Our contingencies, our problems, our troubles, our defects, our sickness and our limitations are all mental fixations (crystallized thoughts) which have so colored and clouded our vision that we are unable to recognize or experience right conditions.

Jesus said: "Be not overcome of evil, but overcome evil with good." Rend the veil. Change your thought. Cleanse your vision. Get a better focus. Reverse the polarity of your faith. Increase your ability to see. See the fact instead of the fable. Look up and not down. Let go and take hold. Declare your Christhood. Adopt a new self and merit good instead of evil.

When you have done these things, then you will be as powerful as you have been weak; as free as you have been bound; as healthy as you have been sick; as rich as you have been poor. "The depth of your valley is the height of your mountain." You will see more and therefore attract more into your experience. Why? Because you always travel in the direction you look. You always attract what you see. You always find what you are looking for.

That is why Jesus said that a man's enemies shall be they of his own household. The "household" is your consciousness and the enemies are your own negative reactions to the untoward things that happen to you. They are your own powers turned downward toward appearance instead of upward toward God. You have forgotten the fact and accepted the fable. Jesus said: "Look up, for your redemption draweth toward you." There are always "two in the field; the one shall be taken and the other left."

What are these "two" which are "ever in the field?" They are the possibilities of good and evil, the blessings and the curses, the fact and the appearance, the Real and the unreal.

Then, how shall we change evil and imperfect manifestations? How shall we attract good instead of evil? How shall we use the Christ Mind instead of the human mind? We have the answer in the scriptures: "Turn away your faces from all your abominations, and return unto me, seeking my face." We do this by withdrawing our attention, and thus, our power, from the negative appearance (refusing to have anything to do with it in our thought), and by contemplating and embodying the spiritual fact—the Truth as it is ·and ever remains in Christ.

The Law works in the exact way we use it. It is to us what we are to It. If it works for limitation when we are wrongly related to It (when our thought is turned downward toward self), then It will work for abundance when we are rightly related to It (when our thought is turned upward toward God).

The human mind of itself is incapable of thinking straight. Drawing its evidence and conclusions from the surface and appearance of things, it thinks from the standpoint of limitation, instead of from that of plenty. When it is sad, it is because it forgets the ever present help of God. When it is sick, it forgets the Man Inside Who always is well. When it is impoverished, it forgets the rich treasures of the Kingdom within.

In other words, the human ·mind forgets what is right and remembers only the wrong. Everything is in reverse. When trouble comes, it tries to meet it with ceaseless misdirected and purposeless activity of mind and body. It runs wildly here and there, seeking a way of escape. It looks to personality and material things for its salvation.

Baffled in one direction, it seeks, another equally bad. Failing in one plan, it adopts another of no more help. Being sensitive to trouble and misery, it absorbs them into the whole being until there is room for nothing else. Feeding on the husks of. the surface, the human mind finally wears itself, out and the whole nervous system is bro ken down.

So, having seen the human mind in some of its most destructive and disrupting moods, we naturally ask, "How can the direful influence and the captivity of this mind be broken and its baleful effects removed?" The answer is this: By turning away from the appearance; by quieting the mind and establishing yourself in the spiritual fact. In order to become free, you must not only reverse your thoughts, and thus set the sight of the mind in the right direction, but you must also learn to think from the Center (standpoint of Truth) instead of from the surface, or the human mind.

This is what we mean by streamlining mental action, and what the metaphysician calls "the parting of the ways by which you separate yourself from the undesirable and enter into the Kingdom of the desirable. It is the means of purposefully directing this seeing sense of the mind into the realm of Divine Reality. It is, therefore, the gateway beyond which lie all the Infinite resources of God and the Perfection which He has ordained for all men from the beginning."

Now, take your concordance and hunt up all the Bible references to the Kingdom of God and the Kingdom of Heaven, and you will soon see why this is the quickest and most direct route to everything good that is lacking in your life. You will see why it is that when you center yourself in It, nothing but Good can get into your life.

Jesus' teachings on the Kingdom of God seem paradoxical. In one instance, He referred to It as a coming kingdom: . . . "until the Kingdom of God shall come". At another time He referred to It as already here: "The Kingdom of God is within you ". At still another time He referred to It as a present possession: "Blessed are the poor (detached) in Spirit, for theirs is the Kingdom of Heaven." In yet another place, He said that It must be sought: "Seek ye first the Kingdom of God, and His righteousness; and all these things shall be added unto you."

And again he said: "The Kingdom of God cometh not with observation."

God's Kingdom is not a visible kingdom with certain boundaries like the British empire, a colony or a province over which a human king presides, but the invisible locality of His immediate Presence. It is not on yon hill nor in Jerusalem. It is not in one place more than another; not in one person more than another, not in one church more than another. It is anywhere and everywhere at the same time — all of It. It is wherever you are, in the same way that a radio program is wherever you are, although it does not come into manifestation until you tune in.

If God is Omnipresent, then His Kingdom is omnipresent — everywhere equally present. It is within all, through all, above all and under all, and may be entered by any one who has a child-like receptivity. "Whosoever shall not receive the Kingdom of God as a little child [be receptive and responsive to it] shall in no wise enter therein." "Except one be born anew [changed — having put off the old man], he cannot see [experience] the Kingdom of God."

In his parable on the seed and the leaven, Jesus pointed out that the Kingdom of God is the most vital force in Nature. In man, in the same way, the germ, or vitality, is in the seed. It grows in him through his recognition and realization of Its presence. Just as "the seed springeth up" and "the earth bringeth forth fruit" when soil and seed are perfectly integrated, so man, when he synchronizes his power with God-power, will furnish the condition to accomplish anything good he desires.

That is why St. Paul said, "I can do all things through Christ which strengtheneth me." When God-power and manpower (which are native to one another) are united, then is fulfilled the promise that "I will give thee the desires of thine heart."

This, then, is the ·gift we are asked to "stir up" — the Kingdom of God in man, the vitality in the seed. It is already there waiting a chance to grow, to come forth. It is the great benefit, the great good, ·waiting to be revealed — the rich treasure hidden in the field; the lost coin; the net that was cast into the sea; the pearl of great price; the leaven in the meal, the power in the mustard seed.

It is the Man Inside, Who is always well; that quickening influence which called Lazarus from the tomb; the transcendent power that healed lepers, straightened crippled limbs, opened deaf ears and blind eyes, stilled the storm and multiplied the loaves and fishes.

Now, let us turn to another aspect (the permeating influence) of the Kingdom of God, which Jesus likened unto leaven or yeast. "The Kingdom of Heaven is like unto leaven, which a woman took, and hid in three measures of meal, till the whole was leavened." Why do you suppose Jesus used the symbolism of three in this instance? Why not two measures of meal, or four, or six?

There were two very definite reasons: First, He was talking to peasant people who had very little understanding of Truth. He must use language which the least of them could understand. An epha of flour (three measures) was the amount used for an average baking. Every peasant woman knew that, and so none would miss the truth He was setting forth.

Then, second, He was showing them the relationship between the Kingdom of God and their individual lives, and making it plain that they must be kept in perfect harmony, functioning as a unit.

The three measures of meal are also symbolical of the three phases of man's being — body, mind and spirit. Just as leaven will permeate and transform a lump of inert, heavy dough into a fragrant and spongy mass, so the Kingdom of God, if given a chance, will permeate and transform a man's entire life. It will not only conquer his ills and solve his problems, but will bring to him all the things necessary for a full, prosperous and perfect life.

"The Kingdom of Heaven is like unto leaven." And how does leaven work? It works in silence and by contagion. Like all other mighty forces, it is noiseless and deep. It transforms life, not by human aid or effort, but by its own inherent power. When Jesus taught us to pray: "Thy Kingdom come . . . on earth, as it is in Heaven," He was not talking about a material utopia that was to be ushered in by human effort, collective bargaining and moral rearmament, social legislation or international cooperation, or to be accomplished by making all men Episcopalians, Roman Catholics, Methodists or Lutherans.

"The Kingdom of God cometh not by observation." It does not come just because we think in a certain way, pray in a certain way or worship in a specified manner. It is not here because we outlaw war, gambling, crime or liquor. The Kingdom of God is within us, waiting to be released. It is inward and invisible like the leaven in the dough. It cannot be seen or touched — "cometh not by observation."

The Kingdom of God is intangible but Real, and worketh by contagion "until the whole is leavened." It spreads (through our realization) in every direction until it has included everything good within itself.

And who are the members of the Kingdom of Heaven? They are—the GOD-CENTERED: Those who have established themselves in the consciousness of His Presence. The DETACHED: Those who are in the world but not of it. The self-renounced, the self-surrendered, the impersonal, the one-pointed, the single-eyed.

They are those disciplined from the center: the changed, the converted, the obedient, the receptive. They are those undivided in heart: the God-directed. the reconciled, the God seekers, the relaxed, the poised, the pure in heart, the naturalized in God.

Yes, the requirements are high but membership is forever. It is the guarantee of everything good here and hereafter.

RELEASING THE KINGDOM OF GOD

Our next inquiry in this realm leads into that part of the Kingdom which vitally concerns you and me. When Jesus said that "The Kingdom of God is within you," He did not mean that it was in any part of the body, as the heart, brain or solar plexus. He meant that It was within your soul, or True Self. St. Paul said, "Christ in you the hope of glory," and, again, "Let Christ be formed in you."

Thus, to enter the Kingdom of Heaven, you need only to realize God's: Presence as a Reality in your own soul. This means that you must fill your consciousness so full of God's Presence and Power that there is no room for the presence and power of anything else.

In his book "TRUTH IDEAS OF AN M.D.," Dr. C. O. Southard says that "a consciousness of anything is a mental awareness of it, a deep feeling that it is true, or an inner sensation of contact with it. The state is entirely a mental one and does not depend upon any position of the body, or upon ceremonies.

"A consciousness seldom comes suddenly; we usually arrive at it by orderly steps, after due mental preparation. A consciousness begins as an idea that is implanted in the mind, just as a seed is planted in the ground. Thoughts are then directed toward this idea and concentrated upon it, thus nourishing it as the rains supply food to the growing plant. The idea draws these thoughts to itself, expanding continually until it fills the mind and becomes a mental state that governs all thinking. This is the parable of the mustard seed that grew to be a tree large enough for the birds to roost in.

"Implant in your mind the idea that God is always with you; that it is He who is working through you, no matter what you may be doing. Then concentrate your thoughts upon this ideal refer to it as a fact in all you think or do, an d you will find it growing until you will feel as a great truth that He is actually right with you. You will then be in the full consciousness of the Kingdom of God.

"This is the realm of all good. When you establish your self in this consciousness you become aware that the source of all good is within you, just where the Master taught us that it is. God is our supply of everything, health, happiness, abundance and love. These are all in that inner Kingdom, waiting to be brought forth. You must become conscious of God as All-Good right within you before you can demonstrate these things in the outer."

That is why Jesus told you to put the Kingdom first and why it is not only the quickest way to everything good, but the quickest way out of everything evil. You must first make yourself a magnet for the things that seem to be missing from your life.

The Kingdom is the Magnet, and if you get your mathematics wrong then your life will add up wrong. If you seek things before you seek God, then nothing will come out right. Your prayers will be clouds without rain. You will meet with frustration, delay and defeat. The Kingdom Idea, on the other hand, works "until the whole is leavened" — until everything in your life is adjusted, renewed, transformed and thrown into balance.

Now, let us think for a few moments about the words "His righteousness." "Seek ye first the Kingdom of God, and His righteousness; and all these things shall be added unto you." Why "His righteousness?" What is righteousness? There is a right side and a wrong side to everything, and to seek "his righteousness" is to keep yourself on the right side of life — judging not according to appearances, but according to the Reality behind them.

When you put the Kingdom of God first, then you are always right. Then the Universe is behind you, working with you and through you for the things you need. It also means having faith in God as the Source of all your good.

You seek the Kingdom of God by establishing yourself in the Consciousness of His Presence. You seek His righteousness by keeping yourself on the right (true) side of the Law — having faith in Him as the Source of all your good and letting His Wisdom guide you in all that you think, say and do.

The magnet, of course, is your consciousness of the Presence of God (Kingdom of Heaven) and the result is the fulfillment of your desires—"all these things shall be added unto you." Thus, those who are in the Kingdom find that Life works with them. Those outside the Kingdom find that life works against them.

Now, turn again to the key at the beginning of this book and you will see why it is that the quickest way to the fulfillment of your desires is to make them of no importance in your thought. If the Kingdom of God, as Jesus said, works like leaven (by its own inherent power), and contains all things within Itself, then to seek "things" is to put the manifestation before the Power that manifests. It is to put the egg before the chicken, the oak before the acorn, the effect before the Cause. It is to diminish power and to lose ground.

The only important thing in Life is God, and to have Him in the possessive case is to have everything else in abundant measure.

Jesus made this very clear in His Sermon on the Mount: "Take no thought for your life (have no anxiety or concern about it), what ye shall eat, or what ye shall drink; not yet for your body, what ye shall put on." And, again, He asked: "Which of you by taking thought (using the human mind) can add one cubit unto his stature?" He answered this by saying: "If ye then be not able to do that thing which is least, why take ye thought for the rest?"

Then He illustrates the principle of involuntary living (laborless activity) by showing how God feeds and cares for the birds and fowls of the air, and the lilies of the field, which toil not nor spin, and then tells us to "Seek ye first the Kingdom of God, and His righteousness; and all these things shall be added unto you." How shall they be added? Without effort, without thought and without using the human mind. "Your Heavenly Father knoweth that ye have need of all these things"; and, "It is His pleasure to give you the Kingdom."

How does He give you the Kingdom? He gives It through your consciousness of It. When you have stopped taking thought about "things," having made things of no importance in your thought, then you are naturalized in God. Then the Christ Mind takes possession of your mind, and not only saves you from whatever you need to be saved from, but fills every vacancy and vacuum in your life.

The Laws of the Kingdom are always self-acting. They become active in you just to the degree that you think with the Mind of Christ and let His Wisdom guide you. Get your center right, says Jesus, and everything else will be right. You do not need to demonstrate houses, money, automobiles, happiness and health, because these already exist for you. Your part is simply to accept them. Under the laws of the Kingdom you do this by establishing yourself in God's ever active Law of Good.

St. Paul said: "Awake thou that sleepest, and arise from the dead (crystallized thoughts of the human mind), and Christ shall give thee light." In other words, act as if you already are in the Kingdom of God — awake and you shall know that you are. When the human mind tells you that you are poor, handicapped, captive or sick, refuse to accept it. Still the human mind; BELIEVE and you will realize the wonderful promise — you will realize that you are rich, free, well, perfect.

CAPITULATION

Since the Kingdom of God is the Cause of all good, and is native to us (written in our inward parts), then to give it pre-eminence in our thought will cause all things to work together for our good:

What is lost will be found. What is missing will be supplied. What is sick will be made well. What is crooked will be made straight. What is rough will be made smooth. What is abnormal will be made normal. What is wrong will be made right. What is bound will be made free. What is complicated will be made simple. What is impossible will be made possible. What is hidden shall be revealed. What is weak will be made strong. What is poor will be made rich.

"I beseech you therefore, brethren, to present your bodies a living sacrifice." Give your body to the Kingdom of God. Give It your brain to think with, your eyes to see with, your ears to hear with, your voice to speak with, your limbs to act with. Then nothing but good will enter your life. Disease will vanish before It like shadows before the dawn. Problems and difficulties will dissolve like snow before the summer sun.

Only give up your life and affairs to the Kingdom of God and "He will manifest Himself through you as all the good you can imagine." Your needs will be supplied in such abundance that "there will not be room enough to receive them."

All the author asks is that you try this out. Start today by establishing yourself in God's Presence. Take the thought:

"God In me Is the only Presence and Power In my life. I am conscious of this presence at all times and under all circumstances, and know that It is guiding me In every thought, word, decision and act, and that It Is filling me with all good."

Fix this idea in your mind; direct all your thoughts to it. If you will do this, it will expand quickly and your consciousness will bring back rich rewards from the Greater Kingdom within you.

Remember, however, that there is nothing in the Kingdom of Heaven but God, and to put anything before Him is to be deprived of that thing. Make your desire of no importance, therefore, and it will come back to you in a most unexpected manner. "With God all things are possible," and to be with God is to be in His Kingdom — to be establish in the consciousness of His Presence.

It is tile quickest way to everything good and the quickest way oat of everything evil.

II
Awakening the Power

"A wake thou that sleepest, . . . and Christ shall give thee Light."

What a nightmare! What dour times! What a chaotic world! What nebulous problems! What trials! What griefs! What difficulties! What suffering! Yes, it is terrible what you have had to go through in recent years. There is scarcely a person whose world has not been turned upside down. There is scarcely an adult who has not had terrific adjustments to make. The frustration, limitation, disappointment and chagrin have been almost more than you could bear.

In calm weather it seemed as though you were spiritually strong and equal to any need. You thought you were superior to such things; immune, so to speak. When life flowed along in its accustomed course you thought that nothing in the outside world could touch or hurt you. Then the gates of hell opened, and you found yourself engulfed in a strange chaos which some one else had made. You found that your spiritual roots were not as deep as you had supposed.

Unconsciously you found yourself swept away, helpless, shattered, crushed. You wondered for the first time if your religion really worked, or if it was an empty conventionality, and whether you should try to save it or let it go. Then you prayed longer and worked harder than ever before. You tried everything you had been taught and everything others suggested. You tried prayers and affirmations by the score, but nothing seemed to help. If anything your problems became worse instead of better.

Why, you asked, should such things happen to you? You are a Truth student. You have taken ail the best courses, studied all the best books and meditated for years. You always had thought of yourself as different from those conventional Truth students whose religion was only a form. Why, then, could you not meet such problems? Where now were the results of your accumulated knowledge, your years of study, your practice and your faith?

> "If after all that we have lived and thought,
> All comes to nought —
> If there be nothing after Now,
> And we know that — why live?"

It is, of course, a serious turn in a person's history when his life tumbles in and his beliefs fail. But the real crisis in the contemporary scene is not the catastrophe, but our willingness to be baffled, discredited and frustrated in our minds. The real tragedy in such barren times is not the thing that happens to us individually, but our failure to realize it and utilize it as an opportunity to add another dimension to our life — the dimension of depth. The unsolved problem, however complicated, does not denote a dead-end street, but lack of wisdom. When wisdom is perfect, the problem will disappear of its own accord.

Spurgeon once said: "A high character might be produced, I suppose, by continued prosperity, but it has seldom been the case. Adversity, however it may appear to be our foe, is our true friend. And after a little acquaintance with it, we receive it as a precious thing — the prophecy of a coming joy." In our present state of consciousness God does not look after us by shielding us from great difficulties, but by making us face the hazards and then enlarging our consciousness to meet the tests which they put upon us.

Truth of itself does not offer us escape from difficulty, but the means by which to face and outwit the difficulty. Would you have it otherwise? Then you would become weak and stunted in your growth—you would lose the joy and zest of living. Just as muscles grow and airplanes rise by resistance, so our spirits develop skill and power by the hardships we face and overcome. James, the brother of Jesus, understood this perfectly when he said: "Let it be all joy to you, my brothers, when you undergo tests of any sort; because you have the knowledge that the testing of your faith gives you the power of going on in · hope but let this power have its full effect, so that you may be made complete, needing nothing."

Someone has said that the "way to meet the blocked passageways of life so as to give them meaning is to learn to see on each closed door a hand pointing farther on. When you get there, and that door is closed, look for the same hand. If you, do not become discouraged, but learn something of value from each failure, the right door will one day swing open."

Emerson said: "It is not the size of the problem that defeats us but the ignorance, inferiority and shallowness of our minds." The victorious life must have depth as well as height, breadth as well as length. In great difficulties the shallows will not do. To be strong in danger and confident in disaster, we must have not only breadth of vision and endurance of courage, but we must be willing to let life teach us by its tests.

Instead of seeing our extremities as the failure of our faith, we should see them as greater opportunities, not only to prove old. truths but to deepen our faith and to enlarge our consciousness. That is why difficulties are given to us, and if we fail to learn the lessons they come to teach, then they will have no meaning for us.

> "If all my ships go out t o sea
> And never come back home to me,
> If I must watch from day to day
> An empty waste of waters gray —
> Then I shall fashion one ship more
> From bits of driftwood on the shore;
> I'll build that ship with toil and pain
> And send it out to sea again."

What resolution the poet expresses in this verse! What courage! What vision! What faith! It is the gospel which needs insistence in this very hour. When life slows down and a} most stops, when disappointment, frustration and disaster come, there is just one thing to do—build another ship and send it out to sea again. On every closed door see the Hand of God pointing to another door farther on, and eventually you will see the green light and go through. The promise is that "In due season we shall reap, if we faint not."

IS IT THE ELEVENTH HOUR IN YOUR CASE?

Then just one thing is necessary: Be more steadfast than ever before. No matter what may be happening on the surface cling to your faith in God. Be dauntless. Be unafraid. Refuse to budge. Refuse to let go. Look up. Lift up. Think up. Work up. Assume the attitude of Job: "Though he slay me, yet will I trust him." Be willing to stay awake in the garden. Be willing to watch with Him. Be willing to acknowledge Him in all your ways. Be willing to go all the way to the Cross. Put your trust in Him.

Seek the deepest as well as the Highest, and, in His own way, God will give you the ability to outwit, outmaneuver or surmount every problem in your life. You can count on it.

"But I have tried all that," you say, "and it doesn't work. It is so dark now I cannot see my way out. I am at the end of my rope." So much the better. "Man's extremity is God's opportunity." Neither can the man digging a tunnel see his way out, but he never knows when the next stroke of his pick will bring him into the light. You say that you have tried an this, but have you stopped thinking about yourself and your needs long enough to let God work out His plan through you. Maybe you haven't surrendered everything that you are. Maybe you haven't controlled your thoughts so that they deal only with permanent things.

It doesn't make any difference, you see, what you have done nor how much you have done; if you haven't obtained results, then you haven't done enough. You have left undone those things which ought to have been done, and it is your duty to find out what they are.

> "Genius, that power which dazzles mortal eyes,
> Is oft but perseverance in disguise.
> Continuous effort, of itself, implies,
> In spite of countless falls, the power to rise.
> 'Twixt failure and success the point's so fine
> Men sometimes know not when they touch the line.
> Just when the pearl was waiting one more plunge,
> How many a struggler has thrown up the sponge!"

"Fit square, polish thyself," says Richard C. Trench. "Thy turn will come. Thou wilt not lie in the way. The builders will have need of thee. The wall has more need of thee than thou hast of the wall." What are these paroxysms, which cause the embryonic chick to peck violently at his shell? What is this darkness which encompasses him and threatens his life? Is it a prophesy of his doom, the final word of nature concerning his fate? By no means. It is the Power of God seeking to break the shell and release the chick into the broader life awaiting him.

You say that it is dark and that your plight is desperate. So it is, but do not forget that it is in the darkness that Christ shines the brightest. It is against the night that the Guiding Star shines clearest. It is against weakness that strength is made perfect. It is against failure that success is born. It is against sickness that health is made manifest. It is against poverty that riches are revealed. It is against sorrow that joy comes. It is when every other door has closed that God opens a new one.

BIG DIFFICULTIES ARE YOUR BIG MOMENTS

Why, then, should you go to pieces when your little fragmentary experimentations and efforts fail? Why should you become despondent, defeated and depressed? Why should you allow your failure to lead you to doubt God? Haven't you learned that the big difficulties are your big moments in the Divine Scheme, and that the only sin in failure is your willingness to believe in failure—to accept it?

Suppose that finally you do have to employ a lawyer to settle a dispute. Suppose that finally you do have to borrow at the bank the money which you hoped and tried to demonstrate. Is there any spiritual recrimination due in such decisions other than the blow to your spiritual vanity and pride? Does your inadequacy prove anything more than your need of a greater faith and a greater consciousness of God's Presence?

In the old days you had good results and you liked to tell others of them. You enjoyed impressing them with the profundity of your thought, your understanding and of your demonstrations. There was very little outside interference in those days and it was easy to get through. But now you have entered a new cycle and you are ready to take another step. You are ready to add another dimension to you r life. You not only have bigger problems and greater difficulties to meet, but a bigger and more destructive community thought to heal. The circuits are now jammed with static and confusion. Inarticulate cries fill the air.

You have entered the most tragic hour of the world's Gethsemane Destruction, peril and death are riding high. Frustration, sorrow and disaster are the common lot of millions. You now are in the position of the Psalmist when he prayed: "Out of the depths have I cried unto Thee, O Lord." You are like the prodigal in the far country.

Much that once you held dear now is being swept away. Nothing is as it was. The old is giving way to the new. Limitation, restriction and depression are everywhere. Privileges that we once took for granted are now denied. Simple things have become complicated. Ordinary things have become rare. Good things have become inferior. Luxurious things have become extinct. The important things now are not jeweled crowns, fabulous salaries, palaces, expensive cars, country homes, stocks and bonds, but power to cope with life and strength equal to our needs.

It is as if some vandal had broken into Life's Show Window at night and shifted all the price tags. As one woman said recently, "Values change so rapidly nowadays that no one can keep up with them, let alone anticipate them." That is true of the outer world of things, but there is one value that does not change—"CHRIST IN YOU THE HOPE OF GLORY"—the same yesterday, today and forever.

THE UNCHANGING POWER

What a comfort it is to know that in a world where nothing remains the same, there is something within us an d instantly equal to every need, which never changes—something on which everyone can rely with absolute certainty in every emergency.

Yes, my friend, we are turning once again to the Father's House, to the values which are eternal. Our selfish, smug complacency has gone. We are falling back upon these enormous resources and locked up abilities which we have never used. We are going to bring out that Bigger Possible Man who has never been found by us. We are going to get at Him, stir Him up, call Him out. We are no longer satisfied with the man we are, but claim the man we are capable of being.

The demand of the hour is for a power not our own and, by the Grace of God, we are going to find It. We are going to find It, not by the little, feeble demands of "bread and fish," but by an unconditional surrender of the whole man to God. Whether the problem be great or small, the principle of correction and creation always is the same: "LET THIS MIND BE IN YOU, WHICH WAS ALSO IN CHRIST JESUS."

"LET," do you hear? "Let this Mind be in you" by RECOGNITION (ascribing all power to It), by BELIEF (knowing no other), by ACCEPTANCE (admitting no contrary evidence), by REALIZATION (calling upon It in every need), by SELF-DENIAL (living in tune with God), by DEVELOPMENT (thinking positively and constructively), by EMBODIMENT (submitting It to every test).

"That is wonderful," you say, "and I believe every word of it, but I just cannot make it work." Of course, you cannot MAKE It work, and as long as you try, you will fail. You will fail because you are working in reverse. You are working from the wrong end. You are using a voluntary instead of an involuntary principle. Jesus said: "My Father worketh hitherto, and I work." His method was conformity to the Divine Will. As He got Himself out of the way, God did everything through Him. His words, "I WORK," mean the control of thought and the denial of self.

God works for us when we work with Him. He takes possession of us when we have purified our minds, when poisonous things no longer creep into them. He gives to us when we lose the sense of need.

AWAKENING THE POWER

"Of mine ownself I can do nothing: the Father within, He doeth the work." It is a process of "letting go" and "letting God," as when Isaiah said: "The government shall be upon His shoulder." Notice the word "shall." A *shall* is a command. It is a "must" and until we recognize that fact and apply it to our lives, we shall get few results from our work. "It is no longer I that live, but Christ liveth in me:" The Power operates through our conscious Christ-hood, and It does not operate in any other way.

God works with us when we work with Him. Will the light come on when you turn the switch? Will water flow when you turn on the faucet? Will God answer your call when you have His mind? The answer is yes—not in some future time or place, but NOW. It is just a matter of getting yourself out of the way until the work is done. "Simple," you say. Then why don't you do it? Why not put God first? Why don't you get rid of "you" so that the good things can get through?

When St. Paul told Timothy to stir up the gift that was in him, he was telling him to arouse the Power that already was there, to recognize It and to call It forth. "God is able to do for you exceeding abundantly above all that you ask or think, according to the Power that worketh in you." The Power already is there—a sleeping giant within you. It is within you and every individual. You instinctively know It and feel It. It is the undiscovered part of you, your other Self. It is the latent force within you, which until now you have not been able to get hold of.

It is your surplus "life capital"—your unused assets. It is that which, when you cooperate with It, makes the old man new, the sick man well, the poor man rich, the depressed man happy. It is that which, when you trust it, destroys everything that would degrade you, neutralizes everything that would impoverish you, transforms everything that would depress you, and dissolves all things that would defeat you.

It is that which, when you call upon it in faith, increases your efficiency and turns failure into success. It solves your problems and overcomes your difficulties. It develops in you new forces, unlocks new resources. It turns enemies into friends, and it transforms undesirable circumstances. It opens new doors, so that you may become that which you long to be. It fulfills your ambitions and your right desires. It gives, finally, what you want.

The great workings of practical religion are that they change our incomplete lives to what they ought to be. We are tired of bondage, penury, failure, frustration and cramped circumstances, and, like the prodigal son, we want to be free. We want to leave behind us the confusion of the present and the uncertainty of the future. We want to express more and to have more. We want to have more serenity and security than we have ever known. We want more health, more freedom and more prosperity than we have ever had.

Yes, we want the Life and Freedom of Christ, and to "have it mare abundantly." We want a power which we do not now express — power to love, power to decide, power to act, power to create, power to heal; power to remain calm under stress, power to transform, power to endure, power to pray effectively. We want power to solve problems, to be resilient, purposeful and accurate. We want power to really think — power to really live.

Oh, if we just bad the power to rise above this difficult and complicated world! If we just had the power to remain steady when those about us are losing their heads! If we Just had the power to transmute adversity into joy, failure into success! If we just had greater capacity, more endurance, more strength and more energy, what wonderful things we would do! What wonderful heights we would reach! What triumphs we would attain!

Every one has voiced these same thoughts many times, but what is the use of merely talking about them, of wishing, hoping, longing? Why not do something about our deficiencies? Why not turn our dreams into realities?

Jesus said: "All power is given unto me (unto you) in Heaven (mind) and in earth (body)." Can there be more than ALL? Can there be less? Can one person, in reality, possess more than another? Can one have less? Then, why not call out the full Power and harness it to our needs? Why accept less than all — less than completeness? Why not use what we have? Why is there such a discrepancy between the Universal Power of God and the individual power of man? Why is there such a loss in transmission, in stepping it down? Why? Because of man's refusal to identify himself and his daily needs with that power.

Webster defines power as the "ability, whether physical, mental or moral, to act; the faculty of doing or performing something; the capacity for action or performance or for receiving external action or force." What we really need, therefore, is a consciousness and a receptivity equal to the gift.

The Power (all power) is already in manifestation. "The Kingdom of Heaven is at hand." "All things are now ready." It is waiting to serve us and to be to us whatever we choose. To be to us more supply, more strength, more guidance, more happiness, more success. Our part is to harness It and to release It — to express It in our daily lives. And how shall we do that? Through our thoughts, words, acts and faith. "Act as though I am and I will be."

Are you lacking in power? Are you unable to control the conditions and circumstances of your life? Are you denying the Omnipotence of God? Do others seem to have more power than you? Then, take your attention away from your limitations and say to yourself:

"The Power of God in me is my freedom from all weakness, limitation, adversity and fear. His omnipotence is now expressing itself in me In all my all affairs."

Now, supply the missing word in the affirmation that follows, the missing word, of course, representing the fulfillment of your need:

"THE POWER OF GOD IN ME IS THE POWER FOR........................ IN MY LIFE."

If your problem is one of sickness, then insert the word "HEALTH"

If your problem is one of evil, then use the word "GOOD."

If your problem is one of impending failure, then supply the word "SUCCESS."

If your problem is one of financial limitation, then add the word of "PROSPERITY;" and so on.

When you know that God (the Power of Good) is the only power in your life, and that It is manifesting in you and in your affairs now, this minute, then adversity can hold no power over you, cannot affect you. Adversity then will be as irrelevant to you as a man with a sword would be to the atmosphere if a man with a sword should try to slay the atmosphere.

Know, then, that nothing in the outer world can stand against the power of God in you. Know it with all your mind, heart, strength and soul. Know that no one can hurt you, defeat you or complicate your life but yourself.

How simple it all is when we open our lives to the Presence of that Power which is able to do all things — everything that the human mind finds impossible — when we know that "Those that are for us are more than those that are against us." So, let us hold this thought:

"Centered in God, my power is mighty, irresistible, inexhaustible. It is here now, wherever I am and in whatever I may be doing. 'Lo, I am with you always.'

"In every perplexity, problem, pain, sorrow or uncertainty, God in the midst of me is mighty! Mighty to transcend, subdue, and banish every other force in my life.

"Mighty to solve every problem, to heal every disease, to strengthen every thought, to transmute every adversity, to overcome every difficulty, to quicken every faculty.

"Mighty to cleanse my consciousness, to cleanse my vision, to set aside my limitations, to change my nature, to bring out my best — to lead me into a triumphant, happy, successful life."

It is glorious what this Un-Conditioned Power will do for us when we give It a chance, when we allow It to flow through us free and untrammeled. "God is able to do for us exceeding abundantly above all that we ask or think, according to the Power that worketh in us."

Then, why look outside for our good, to persons, influences, conditions and things? Why look to others? There is a right way and a wrong way to do everything, and the right way to demonstrate is to place our order and then stay the mind upon the finished idea while the Power works it out. "So shall my word be that goeth forth out of my mouth: It shall not return unto me void, but it shall accomplish that whereto it is sent."

Staying the mind on the finished idea, without any thought of the "how" or the "when," is advance notice to the Universe that there is one who takes God at His Word. The prayer becomes active and the power goes forth to fulfill itself. Realization releases the power and our word directs it. It is God's guarantee of instant response, and the petitioner will receive what he asks.

Please note, however, that the power is spiritual and not material. Jesus said:

"Seek ye first"—what? fame, fortune, position, houses, lands? No. "Seek ye first the Kingdom of God and His righteousness." The prior condition is righteousness, faith in God and the right use of His Law. That must come first; if you put anything before It you will fail. You are to seek the Kingdom in the same way that you would seek a position, a house or any other thing. You keep hunting until you find It, and when you find It, you move into It and It moves into you.

Jesus said: "Remain within my love;" and, again: "If ye abide in me [keep centered in my consciousness], and my words [spiritual thoughts] abide in you, ask what ye will, and it shall be given you."

What Jesus is saying here is that the Kingdom of God must so completely fill your mind and life that no matter where you go, whom you contact, or in what circumstances you may be, you shall know, see and find the Presence and Power of

God. Giving Him pre-eminence in your mind, you meet Him wherever you are. Therefore, put God first in everything—God first, others second, and self third.

On five different occasions, Jesus said: "He that saveth his life shall lose it: and he that loseth his life for my sake shall find it." He was talking of surrender, which is the first step in every spiritual quest. Before we can live in God, we must die to self. Nothing else will do. Everything else is relative. Before you can find your life. you must lose it; and the more you lose the more you gain.

That sounds like a paradox, but it means simply that the gates of the Kingdom open only to a surrendered life. You must not only surrender your whole mind, soul and body to the Kingdom of God, but translate that surrender into action and submit it to every test. When some problem or contingency arises, you do not say: "What shall I do?" "Whom shall I see?" "Where shall I go?"

You now say, "In this problem, what does God expect of ME?" Then you carry out the expectation. In this turmoil, you ask. "What part does the Kingdom expect me to play?" Then you play it. You seek every opportunity, so, to speak, to bring the Kingdom of God on earth; or, as Jesus said, to "Let your light . . . shine."

Then, what happens to him who sets out to find the Kingdom of God thinking chiefly of "loaves and fishes" (material things)? He does not get them. Why? Because material things are results, not goals. Jesus said that we were to embody the Kingdom of God in our consciousness and to materialize (make it visible) on earth. We were to give it a body to act with, a mind to think with, emotions to feel with. "Thy Kingdom come. Thy will be done on earth (in my experience), as it is in Heaven."

Thus, doing the will of God means giving His Kingdom form and expression in our lives. WHEN? WHERE? In the after life? No! HERE and NOW. It must begin here or we shall not find it there.

There is no hedging on this point, you see, because the Law says that you must meet the requirements before you can realize the result. It is written into the nature of things. You must die to self before you can live with God. You must desire the Kingdom so strongly that, if it were not for the things: to be added, you would still seek it for its own sake.

Does that sound incredible? Then consider the same law as it obtains on the earthly plane. If your position is only a means of getting money, then you will not make a great deal out of it. But if you love your position for the position's sake, if you love it first for the sake of the service you can give, then you will be rewarded with plenty of money. "All these things shall be added unto you."

DON'T OUTLINE

Now, let us consider ways in which we can help God answer our prayers, and ways in which we hinder Him. Let us take up the hindrances. These are legion, but chief among them is the unholy habit of outlining to God the way in which He does His work for us — how He can solve specific problems or meet pressing needs. This plainly is fatal. It is an open acknowledgment of our lack of faith and trust, a denial of His Omnipotence. It is a sure way of delaying our good.

Have we forgotten that "The carnal mind is enmity against God," and that "My thoughts are not your thoughts" nor "your ways my ways?" God demands our trust and confidence and until we give them to Him we cannot expect answers to our prayers. Let the divided mind remember that God is omniscient, omnipotent and omnipresent. God knows how to do it. God is doing it right now. "Faith is . . . the evidence of things not seen."

DO NOT HOLD ON TO THE OLD

Another mistake many make is the unfortunate habit of holding on to the old while trying to demonstrate the new. Most of us are like pendulums, swinging continuously between the good we hope to attain and contemplation of the evil we are trying to expel. We try to demonstrate strength while contemplating weakness. We try to demonstrate health while entertaining thoughts of sickness. We try to demonstrate success while thinking failure.

So, nothing goes right with us. Nothing turns out well. We meet frustration at every turn. People treat us badly and we convince ourselves that we are having a very difficult time. We pray long and frantically but continue to keep our attention on our troubles. We try to practice the Presence of God while holding thoughts of criticism, antagonism, bitterness, hardship, injustice and revenge.

Don't you see the folly of such limp thinking? We not only are misusing and subverting the Power of God, but we are intensifying our adversities and giving them more strength. We are giving them a firmer hold upon us. Worst of all, we are making it impossible for God to help us.

It was St. Paul who spoke of "casting down imaginations (negations) . . . and bringing into captivity every thought to the obedience of Christ." What did he mean? He meant that we were to refuse to entertain human thoughts of distressing conditions, of trouble, and to keep our minds filled with thoughts of God. Instead of thinking weak, limited and miserable thoughts, we can lift our hearts (minds) to Him and think His thoughts after Him.

Now, do not tell me that you are one of those who cannot discipline your thoughts, for I know that you can. How do I know? Because your mind can think only one thought at a time, and you can choose what kind of a thought that shall be. The whole problem, therefore, is one of single vision, or one-pointedness. "If thine eye be single, thy whole body shall be full of light. "

DO NOT CONTRACT THE POWER

A third way in which we hinder God is by contracting and inhibiting His Power. In spite of the fact that "All power is given unto us," men still try to preserve their power and energy by refusing to express it. They believe that power is limited and must therefore be guarded and used sparingly. How, then, shall we correct this erroneous impression? By realizing that man is an individualized center of the One Creative Power and that he radiates power in direct proportion to his proximity to the Divine Presence.

Power, as we have said, is not personal but spiritual, not human but divine. Then what happens to him who tries to hoard his energy? He loses it. Why? Because Power, like muscles, withers and dies. Capacity grows with use and contracts with disuse. Power that is not used becomes dormant. Power that is held back becomes stagnant.

As St. Paul said, "Power belongeth to God." It is His to give and ours to use. It is He who releases it, and if we do not use it, it is wasted.

Now, turn to the first chapter of the Book of Acts, and you will gee when it is that power comes: "You will receive power, when the Holy Spirit is come upon you." When is that? It is when you are centered in God and have His Kingdom in the possessive case. Of such, Jesus said: "The Kingdom of Heaven is theirs," meaning that they have the support of God. They no longer are working against the Kingdom, but are controlled by It.

Why not start today, then, as St. Paul said, "to enlarge the border of your tent?" — to create a capacity that will equal your fondest ambition? Why not start by driving out the belief that you are frail and handicapped, "that you can do only so much, that you must be careful with yourself and save as many steps as possible?"

The antidote for this misconception is the recognition that it is not your power alone that you are using, but your power plus God's Power. Not your limited and distorted sense of life, but God's all-encompassing care and omnipotence. Not your human problems, conflicts, skirmishes, undesirable circumstances, and frustrations, but God's illuminating and ever-present wisdom. Not your hurts, slights, antagonisms and bitterness, but God's transforming, restoring and cleansing love.

It is not disease, fear, pain and worry, but the immanent and ever accessible Body of our Lord. Not your rebellious, incompatible and destructive thoughts, but the enfolding certitude and security of Christ's Mind. Not your ability, not your responsibility; not your duties, not your power—but His.

Don't you see why it is that you must stop limiting your power? Why you must stop telling your subconscious mind that you are old, feeble, tired and limited, and why you must stop wasting energy by watching yourself lest you overdo or overexert? Jesus says: "Look unto God." In other words, keep a positive, one-pointed attitude toward Him and you will never be limited nor lack strength. Know that there is no power but that which is given you from on High and you will draw from the Divine Source all that you can use. It will come to you in such quantities that there will not be room enough to receive it.

"Lift up now your eyes unto the hills" from whence the power comes. It comes through your uplifted thought. "The Son of man hath power on earth to forgive (erase) sins." You have the innate power to bring forth from the Divine Storehouse all that you need. You have the power to forgive yourself and others; the power to heal yourself and others. You have the power to harmonize your mind with God's Mind and thus to live successfully; the power to solve any problems, erase any mistake, to perform any task, to overcome any obstacle, to dissipate any trouble and to dissolve grief. "All power is given unto me in heaven and in earth."

Yes, it is tremendous what happens when you set the Power in action and release It in your life and affairs. It accomplishes things that the human mind never before dreamed possible. That is why Jesus told us to seek the Power first. When you LET the Kingdom of God into your mind, you cease to be temporal and become eternal. Then you have eternal health, eternal peace, eternal joy, eternal prosperity and eternal life. Indeed, then you "find" yourself and everything that belongs to self.

Folk speech has old sayings often heard but worthy of more consideration than many give them, for they deal with basic principles of life. One is: "He who says he can't is usually right." That is, when we say we cannot do a thing, simply because the work seems difficult or beyond our present measure of ability, we rob ourselves of the power which God ever stands ready to give those who say:

"By the power of the Spirit of God which is in me, I can."

Would you tune in to the great creative Consciousness of the Universe and use it for your daily needs? Then center yourself in God by surrendering your human ego to the Divine Presence. Claim your power by using the Great I AM affirmations which Jesus used:

> **"I am a son of God."**
> **"I am the resurrection and the Life."**
> **"I am the door."**
> **"I am the way, the Truth and the Life."**
> **"I am the Light of the World."**
> **Then, too, claim:**
> **"I am Power."**
> **"I am health."**
> **Etc., etc.**

Get your attention off your weakness and put it upon The Power. If the Heavenly Father knows your needs and supplies them before you ask, then why not put yourself in condition to receive them? As we are promised that prayer is answered before it is made, then why so many repetitions? Why not accept the answer; stay your mind on the FINISHED IDEA and call IT into manifestation?

Are there locked passageways in your life which you have not been able to open? Are there problems you have been unable to master? Are there obstacles that seem insurmountable? Then challenge each one with the word of Power:

"Be thou opened, in the Name of Jesus Christ." "Open, in the Name of the King."

You have read and heard those words in many a melodramatic English novel and play. But an Englishman's home is his castle. How can any one enter? Even the constable may gain entrance only under certain conditions: be must have the state authority and it must be imperative that he enter. Then he declares the conditions under which he demands entrance: "In the name of the King."

So we, in praying, give the conditions under which we make our requests — "In the Name of Jesus Christ"; or, in that phrase which is more familiar to us: "Through Jesus Christ our Lord." This is the final authority for our request.

Let us, then, begin today to use this power in all the perplexities, stresses and troubles that beset us. These are but appearances. Just cast these appearances to one side and tell yourself the Truth about yourself. Say it so convincingly that the inner mind will "sit up and take notice:"

"In the Name of Jesus Christ, I command you (the inner mind) to open and listen to what I have to say:

"God Power right now is strengthening, guiding, blessing me.

"God Power is now flowing through me and finding expression in me. I have claimed it and taken it for my own.

"God Power is now released in me. It is changing in me that which needs to be changed. It is bringing forth within me the highest force.

"I expect strength from God-Power only. I rely utterly upon God-Power. God-Power is now in action in me—is acting now—to serve my needs and to fulfill my sincerest and highest desires.

"'I speak not from myself: but the father abiding in me doeth His Works.'"

HELPING GOD HELP US

Now, let us consider some ways in which we can help God answer our prayers. Maybe you have never thought of God as needing help from you in this, but He does.

Before you can go to a new place, you must leave the old one. Before you can live on a higher plane, you must leave the lower. Before a vessel can be filled with new substance, it must be emptied of the old. Before an athlete can run a race, he must lay aside the weights that would impede his progress; he must strip of all that is superfluous. Before a caterpillar can fly, it must leave its cocoon. Before seed can produce, it must be receptive to soil, sunlight, moisture and air.

Before a man can receive richer blessings, he must hold a larger measure in his mind. Jesus said: "With what measure ye mete, it shall be measured to you again." This means that God can only fill the sized measure we bring to him. The Law is positive on this point, and that is where our help and cooperation come in.

If you would receive rich stores from God, then you must be receptive to them. You must not resist them; you must not only have a consciousness greater than your needs, but you must have the right beliefs, or mental equivalents in your mind.

In His Beatitudes in the Sermon on the Mount, Jesus had much to say on the subject of receptivity. The poor (detached) in spirit are to be given the Kingdom of God. The mourners are to be comforted. The meek are to inherit the earth. The hungry and thirsty are to be filled. The merciful are to receive mercy. The pure in heart shall see God. The peacemakers are to be called the children of God.

Our first step in helping God, therefore, is to provide a greater receptivity for His Good. Seeking the Kingdom first means, among other things, seeking to live with the Limitless; expanding the consciousness until it takes on the largest possible view of everything. We do not gain the good things of life by trying to cram them into a small consciousness, but by trying to expand that consciousness.

We must think and live with the unlimited and unconditioned, and harmonize our minds with His Mind. When the outer man declares that a certain thing is impossible, or cannot be accomplished, we must reply:

"With God all things are possible." "It is in me to do it; therefore I can; therefore I will."

The gate is straight and the path is narrow that leads to the Kingdom of God, because only the God-Centered and the OnePointed are admitted therein. You cannot be double-visioned and double-minded—one part positive and the other part negative, in the Father's House. This is so because His House is restricted to the One. There is room only for the Son (True Self). "Acquaint now thyself with Him, and be at peace."

So long as you seek only the good in everybody and everything, you will be in the Kingdom of God and receive only good in return. But, when you divide your mind, allowing it to dwell on that which is not good, you depart from the Kingdom of God. Then you enter into discord, trouble, confusion, limitation, weakness, and, finally, disintegration. Then things begin to fall apart and your good is scattered. Your mind is out of focus, so to speak, and your life is distorted. "Let not that man think that he shall receive any thing of the Lord."

So, how shall we get our scattered selves back together again? St. Paul says by letting "this Mind be in you, which was also in Christ Jesus." "Letting it" by seeking only the Kingdom of God and by entertaining only thoughts of Good. And what is the result of such a fusion? Then everything in our world will begin to improve. Our Creative Power will attract only the best of everything—better conditions, better circumstances, better people, better deals, better opportunities, better health, greater supply and more harmonious surroundings.

Oh, Yes, there still will be mistakes, delays, recessions, disappointments and unpleasant experiences. But you will pay no attention to these seeming inconsistencies. This because you will know that when your subjective recognition is right, everything in your world will be right.

PRACTICE THE PRESENCE OF GOD

One of the quickest ways to develop a greater receptivity toward God is the consistent and habitual practice of His presence in your life. This means uniting yourself with Him, incorporating yourself in Him, embodying Him, opening your mind to Him, abiding in Him. It means filling your consciousness with Him and beholding Him in every person, place, circumstance, condition, need and thing.

God IS Omnipresent—everywhere equally present. Know this. Realize it, and He will show forth His perfection in every part of your world. You will be guided and managed by a Power that knows all, sees all, gives all and works only for your good.

God IS Omnipresent. Involve this idea in your mind. Know that He is in every cell, in every person, problem, place and thing. Expand your consciousness of this idea until it fills every thing and includes all things in your life. Let it fill your body. It will immunize you against sickness.

"There will be no sickness where God is present as health." There will be no poverty where God is present as wealth. There will be no unhappiness where God is present as joy.

PLACE ALL YOUR AFFAIRS LOVINGLY IN GOD'S HANDS

It is not the purpose of this book to perform your work for you, but to show you how to do things for yourself. You grow not by trying to overpower the undesirable things in your life, but by giving them to God, and trusting Him for the perfect outworking of His Law. The only thing God wants from you is the conscious recognition of His Presence, as here, there and everywhere, and your absolute faith in His power as the Source of all your good.

The clear command is, "Cast your burdens upon the Lord." Therefore, place them all in His Hands. Put Him first in every endeavor, problem, enterprise or need.

Are you undecided as to what to do, where to turn? Then place the situation lovingly in God's Hands. Are you experiencing enmity, antagonism, opposition or contention? Then remember that God can change all this for you. Simply place the problem confidently in His Hands.

Do trouble and confusion seem to have the upper hand? Then give them over to Him. Are you suffering reverses in business to the point of desperation? Then trust Him. Have you lost the way? Then know that God can open ways where there is no way. Leave it to Him. Is the situation so bad and the prospect so dark that you cannot see your way through? Then God can bring you out into the Light."

Are you fearful for the life of some loved one or some friend? Then place him lovingly in God's hands and be at peace. Know that with God all things are possible, and that when you place your loved ones and all your affairs and problems in His Hand; you need no longer be worried or fearful.

God not only can, but will solve every problem and meet every need, if you will but leave it with Him. When He (Good) takes hold, evil falls away of its own weight. When we look to God, we are led by God and find that for which we have been looking.

Are you afraid to surrender your life to God for fear He will take something away from you? Then remember this: God takes a way from you only the things that you want to be rid of—your ills and your illusions.

DEPEND UPON THE CHRIST WITHIN YOU
FOR ALL THINGS AT ALL TIMES

The thing that counts in the long run is our absolute dependence upon God, for everything in our lives—feeling His Presence near, admitting Him into every thought, Word, act and enterprise; trusting Him for every thing. "Look unto me, all the ends of the earth, and be ye saved."

"Look unto me" and all the affairs of your life will be brought into harmony with Divine Law. Doubts will disappear, troubles will vanish, right desires will be fulfilled, lack will be changed to plenty; obstructions will be removed, crooked ways made straight, empty places filled, evil dissolved, sickness will give way to health. All things will be worked out in the most satisfying and orderly manner.

It is to your everlasting advantage to trust God with all things in your life. Particularly is it vital to trust Him with yourself—to put yourself in a position where He can direct your thoughts and act upon your affairs.

CHANGE YOUR MIND AND YOU WILL
CHANGE YOUR LIFE

Had St. Paul been talking in the vernacular of the day, he probably would have said: "Be ye transformed by the changing of your mind;" or, "by the changing of your attitudes." The reason why attitudes are so important to a peaceful and successful life, is that they are the agents which direct the forces back of our minds. Indeed, they affect everything in our lives.

Wrong attitudes call forth the worst in life; right attitudes bring out the best. Thus, to turn on the full current of the mind so that it acts constructively upon the whole life, one must think, work, and feel in a joyous and positive attitude toward God. In other words, he must keep his thought so high that nothing low can get into his life.

Again, as Spinoza said, "Substance is plastic and spirit is compelling." Man must know that there is nothing in his life—nothing in his body or affairs, that cannot be changed; that there is nothing on the lower levels of organized existence that is fixed, and nothing that has reached its ultimate Every desirable thing can be increased and every undesirable thing can be decreased, wiped out. By changing our attitudes (ourselves), by acting in harmony with God, we can overcome all unfavorable conditions in our lives; we can increase and improve every undesirable aspect, thereby increasing our capacity to enjoy that which is best.

We always help God, and thus ourselves, by maintaining a joyful, optimistic and positive attitude toward life. The optimistic attitude not only keeps the mind lifted to God, but keeps it fixed upon the larger and best things of life. With this state of mind comes broader purposes, expanding thoughts, richer ideas, better ideals—greater advancement in all ways.

ACT ALWAYS WITH GOD

"Act as though I am and I will be." This means what? It means putting yourself on the right side of every proposition. It means acting always with the stronger, the larger force; the perfect, the positive, the constructive force—acting with the forward moving, the upbuilding the ever-growing. Regardless of what comes into your, life, act always with God, and whatever assails you will invariably come out right. Act always with and for the best and the best will come back to you.

One of the most serious things you can do when things go wrong is to allow yourself to go wrong with them, to surrender to them. Why? Because such attitudes are on the ebb side of life and will land you on your back. Know instead that God is mightier than any circumstance. Then resolve to see things as right and act to make them right, knowing that the Power of God is back of you. You thereby place yourself on the flood side of life. Then everything begins to change for the better.

One principal reason why many fail to realize their good is that they approach it with doubt, with a divided mind. Then the upper story (conscious mind) is working for one thing, while the lower story (sub-conscious) is denying it, thus perpetuating the lack. The mind is thereby divided against itself and is prevented from reaching its goal.

In this condition the consciousness is trying to move in two directions at the same time. The broadcast is choked by static. The power is short-circuited. The affirmations are checkmated by denials. The positive attitude is diluted by a negative attitude. The harvest is checked by drouth. The higher forces are counter balanced by the lower forces, and the prayer comes to naught.

Do you now see why intentions must be protected until the word becomes flesh? Weeds grow without cultivation; not so with roses. If we want the richest blessings of Heaven, then we must act with God. The whole mind must be synchronized, integrated and harmonized with Him.

BE POSITIVE TO YOUR GOOD

"Enter ye in at the strait gate: for wide is the gate, and broad is the way, that leadeth to destruction, and many there be which go in thereat." The invitation, from St. Matthew's gospel, points out two approaches to life and two modes of thinking. One leads to power, riches, renewal and success, while the other leads to weakness, poverty, destruction and failure.

"Choose ye this day whom ye will serve." Jesus said: "Y e cannot serve God and mammon" — the high way or the low way, the desirable way or the hard way. Choose life or death, Heaven or hell. The choice is yours to make. Upon that choice hinges the outcome of your life, whether you live in peace or discord, in success or failure.

The human way, of course, turns down toward negation, trouble, worry, fear censure, falsity and taint. That way magnifies difficulties, embodies within itself practically an the ills that flesh is heir to.

The high, or difficult way, on the other hand, leads up to God, to greater power, larger possibilities, health, a richer life and perpetual increase.

God not only requires that we give Him our minds, but that we keep, them free from an negative, poisonous and destructive thoughts. To enter at "the strait gate" requires that we give up every negative thought, feeling or attitude the moment we perceive it to be negative, and that we continue to alter our point of view and mental behavior until all our thoughts and attitudes are in focus with Him.

The imperative thing, therefore, in developing a greater receptivity toward. God is, not only to be alert against negative suggestions and thoughts, but to make true our minds and characters, and thus our consciousness. If these are weak, limp, disjointed or cramped, then they must be restored and renewed. And how shall we do that? By being positive always to the Good, and by seeing that "every thought and word give expression to the Power that makes for greater things."

This means that you should never give expression to any thought, or react to any suggestion, that checks your power or points backward or downward from your high goal.

Never discuss your troubles or dwell upon the seamy side of things. Never say you do not feel well; never discuss sickness with any one. Refuse to give voice to the statement that you do not sleep or that you are tired. Never say that you are "only human" or that "everything happens" to you. Never indulge in self-pity. Do not expect misfortune; do not "fear the worst."

Never look for defects in yourself or others, and do not call attention to them. Never criticize others and do not hold enmity toward anyone. Never take offense and give none. Never argue and do not condemn conditions.

Never admit that anything is too difficult for you or that it is impossible of accomplishment. Never discount your abilities nor condemn yourself for anything you have done with right motive. Have no remorse and regrets. Never slump mentally.

Never seek "things;" seek God-Power. Never seek vengeance; try to develop understandings. Never try to "use" God; let Him use you. "Take care of fundamentals and demonstration will take care of itself."

III
"God Is . . . A Very Present Help in Trouble"

"Thy shoes shall be iron and brass; and as thy days so shall thy strength be."

"There is a story of an oriental king, who having to take a long journey, gave orders that he must walk on carpet all the way. But the order proved impossible to carry out: not enough carpet could be found or made. The situation was saved by a bright boy's presenting the King with a pair of carpet slippers!

"Many of us would like the roads we have to tread to be covered with carpet. But we don't find them that way; mostly they are not even smooth, but rough and stony.

"The promise of shoes of iron and brass was made to people who had roads of this kind before them. The idea is not of comfort, but of endurance and mastery. It is an assurance from God of ability to travel the road however hard it is.

"The second part of the promise covers all the difficulties the journey may bring.

"How often we begin a day, with its duties and its burdens, perhaps its pain, afraid that we can never get through with it! Well, perhaps we can't if we try to do it ourselves. But why do we try to do it ourselves when God is waiting to help us? 'As thy days, so shall thy strength be.' No day of ours can be too much for us, if we seek God's strength for it. He gives daily strength for daily needs. 'God is a very present help in trouble.' "

HOW TO THINK OF TROUBLE

Maybe you have never thought of your troubles in this light before. We want you to do so now. A trouble is neither person, place nor thing. It has no power to hurt, disturb or upset you except that which you give it through your own troubled mind. The trouble that troubles you is not the trouble that comes to you but the troubled attitude which you entertain toward it. Does that sound involved? Then it means simply that all troubling is of your own making, and that if you did not react to trouble with a troubled mind there would be no trouble in your world.

The serious mistake most people make when adversity strikes is to take the worst possible view of it. Instead of meeting adversity with a calm, self-possessed attitude, they magnify it, brood over it and thus make it a reality. Then comes a confused, chaotic state of mind that is communicated to the whole being. How, then, shall we meet adversity? By definitely refusing to acknowledge it as dire; by refusing to be troubled by it.

Trouble, like all other negative conditions, is self-made. The way to meet it is to change our point of view. The antidote is peace of mind and tranquility, which are born of faith and realization of our true identity with Divine Mind.

"To dispose of your troubles," says Thomas L. Masson, "face them mentally. Never shrink from the mental contact. Gaze out at them calmly. They will at once begin to fade. Remember that it is almost all in your mental attitude. Don't try to solve anything. Don't think. Don't speculate. Don't keep turning and twisting the thing over in your mind, while the horror of it grows. That is cowardly. Just face it mentally, and remember that the laws of the Universe are not going to be changed on your account. They will always work for you when you work with them.

"If you can manage to acquire faith enough to do this, without caring for the consequence, you will be amazed at the re-results."

In an unfinished world like ours there always will be demonstrations to make and prayers to be said. We should start at the bottom, however, if we expect to rise to the top. The demonstration most needed now is the demonstration of God's Presence. Put this "first," said Jesus, "and all these things shall be added unto you." We should begin, therefore, by asking God to open our eyes; to clarify our vision, to change our point of view.

To meet present needs through spiritual means, we must change our position in the law. We must change from the relative to the Absolute. We must ask to see things as they are and not as they seem.

In the relative (human consciousness) man has a certain capacity for trouble, doubt, fear, worry, grief, unhappiness, uncertainty; hatred, revenge, jealousy, envy and selfishness. In the Absolute (God-Consciousness) there is nothing for such thoughts, moods and emotions to work with. "If ye are in Christ, ye are above the law and not subject to it."

Everyone has problems of one kind or another, but how problems affect us individually depends entirely upon our attitude toward God and our position in the law. If we are walking away from the Light, as was the case of the prodigal son, then the shadows (troubles) will fall in our path, and we shall have to meet them. If we are walking toward the Light, then shadows will fall behind. In that case they will not hurt us. It is obvious, therefore, that it never is the trouble that we have to change but our attitude and reaction toward it.

In the Christ Consciousness, the evils of the relative are neutralized by the Good of the Absolute. The problems change when we change our relations to them. When we put God first in our minds, then everything will be changed automatically for us. Like Zaccheus, Mary Magdalene and the others after they had met Christ, we shall never again see and feel things in the same way as before. We shall say, with Dean Howells after he had met Tolstoy: "I can never again see life in the way that I saw it before I met him."

There is an old saying that "when fate throws a dagger at you, there are two ways to catch it: either by the blade or the handle." The plain truth about everyone is that some kind of trouble or difficulty is unavoidable. The choice we have to make is not between trouble and no trouble, but between acquiesence in trouble and the strength and security of a God-centered mind. The question to be faced is not whether trouble strikes, but whether we are going to allow it to dominate us. Are we going to let it unmake us, or are we going to transmute it into a song? The dagger by and of itself is harmless.

Like the dagger of misfortune, sorrow and defeat, the thrown dagger will do to us only what we permit it to do. It has both the power to cut and the power to defend, depending upon how we use it, and whether we catch it by the handle or by the blade.

The reason a poised mind is indispensable to successful living is that it cushions us against the shocks. It bears the same relation to human difficulties as shock-absorbers on an automobile do to a rough road. Equipped with shock-absorbers, the jars and jolts are absorbed and do not reach the occupants of the car. Rough places are made smooth and difficult places made easy.

Jesus said: "My yoke is easy and my burden is light!" It makes a world of difference, you see, whether trouble and difficulty are allowed to shock you or whether you have a mental and physical shock-absorber which will ease you over the bumps, big or little. Make the poised mind your shock-absorber.[1]

While Emerson's library was burning at his home in Concord, his friend Louisa May Alcott rushed over to him to express sympathy for the loss of his most cherished possessions—his books. She found him serene and poised, watching the flames devour his priceless volumes, many of them autographed copies of books by the world's greatest writers. Although he must have felt his loss keenly, he was as calm as if he were sitting in his library reading. He even could find something to admire in the flames.

"Never mind, Louisa," said he to his sympathetic friend; "see what a beautiful blaze it makes. We'll enjoy that now." Miss Alcott said she never forgot the lesson. From it she learned always to look for something beautiful and helpful even in her disappointments and losses.

THE POISED MIND

One of St. Paul's greatest weapons of defense was his affirmation, "None of these things move me." Calmness is one of the most priceless possessions. It is the poise of a great

---

1 From *You Can But Will You*. Orison Swett Marden.

soul at peace with itself, with the world and with its ideals. It is the glow of a God-centered life that is self-contained self-maintained, self-reliant, and self-controlled. It is the concentrated stillness of the universe ready to spring into action when any emergency appears. The poised mind is ever at the helm—always clear, always cool, always equal to the need.

What the poised man will do and how he does it matters not. He rests confidently in the strength of an inside power, knowing that "one with God is a majority"—that fate never puts an obstacle in his path which the Spirit cannot remove. He does not fight irritating influences and innuendoes from the outside. Neither does he forget himself so far as to retaliate. He knows that nature has but one offensive weapon-the boomerang. He knows that no one can injure another without being injured in return—today, next month, next year, somewhere, somehow, sometime.

It is the Law. Life always balances her books. No one ever escapes the unreconciled injuries or wilful hurts that he inflicts. We punish ourselves. Thus the poised mind always can face calmly the most trying trial, undaunted and undismayed. He can view the worst that can happen to him with a stout heart and steady nerve, and say: "So what! I will build another ship and send it out to sea again."

"Insure yourself against future needs," is a slogan of the day. We have insurance against accident, liability, tragedy and loss. Now, think what it would mean to be insured against the loss of health through sick thoughts; against the loss of supply through poverty thoughts; against the damage to brain structure through temper; against the corrosion of nerve cells and body tissue through worry; against the loss of prestige and initiative through fear, against the loss of mental and physical force through anger, depression, jealousy, envy and revenge.

There IS such an insurance, and it is to be found in the grace and power of a poised mind. When the soul is poised, then, no matter how violent the shock nor how awful the trial, the mind will remain calm, unhurt and undisturbed.

HARNESSING THE EMOTIONS

"For each bad emotion," says Elmer C . Gates, "there is a corresponding chemical change in the body. Every good emotion makes a life-promoting change. Every thought which enters the mind is registered in the brain by a change in the structure of its cells. The change is a physical change more or less permanent.

"Anyone may go into the business of building his own mind for an hour each day, calling up pleasant memories and ideas. Let him summon feelings of benevolence and unselfishness, making this a regular exercise like swinging dumb-bells. Let him gradually increase the time devoted to these psychical gymnastics until it reaches sixty or ninety minutes per diem. At the end of the month he will find the change in himself surprising. The alteration will be apparent in his actions and thoughts. It will have registered in the cell structure of his brain."

God did not intend that man be the victim of destructive passions and harmful emotions, but that he overcome them with a superior force. The antidote lies within ourselves, but it must be uncovered, cultivated and used. "BE NOT OVERCOME OF EVIL," said St. Paul, "BUT OVERCOME EVIL WITH GOOD."

In other words, supply the alkali for the acid: For hate supply love. For despondency supply cheer. For pessimism supply optimism. For discord supply harmony. For sickness supply health. For fear supply faith. For anguish supply peace. For the negative supply the positive. Apply the alkali and the acid will disappear.

It makes no difference how violent the emotion may be, there is no reason why one should ever be thrown off balance and shattered by it. No reason, except that of one's own choosing, why anyone should ever be worried, fearful, unhappy, depressed or sad for a single instant. Why not? Because he always has with him the mental remedies. All he needs do is to apply the antidote and the poisonous thought will instantly be neutralized.

There is no water however dirty that cannot be purified by chemistry, and there is no mind so crippled and polluted by negative thoughts that it cannot be purified by positive thoughts.

In metaphysics we call this process the law of counter suggestion. This means simply, as Jesus pointed out, the counteracting and purifying of destructive thoughts that pollute the consciousness by supplying their opposites. We do this as we would regulate the temperature of hot water, by turning on the cold faucet. When, for instance, anger is in the ascendancy, poisoning and overheating the body, we turn on the peace thought. This cools and equalizes the forces of the body. In the presence of peace, the heat generated by anger is quickly dissipated.

Anyone has the power (if he will but use it) not only of controlling his thinking, emotions and passions, but of regulating his life and maintaining his balance. This power he possesses at all times and under under all circumstances.

When we watch our reactions, control our emotions and guard our thoughts with the same care that we guard our money, then the problem of evil shall have been solved. Armed with a poised mind, the peace which passeth understanding, it will not only be impossible for harmful suggestions to torture us or even disturb our peace of mind, but it will be unnecessary to longer deny their existence.

Does that sound incredible? Too good to be true? Well, try it and see. In times past we attempted to drive evil from our lives with will power and force. Jesus said, Counteract it. Counter suggest it. Be your own mental chemist. "Physician, heal thyself." "Be not overcome of evil, but overcome evil with good." Change the thought. Expel negatives with positives. Empty by filling. Neutralize the acids with alkalis.

Do it yourself. Be your own physician. Use what God has given you. You do not need a psychiatrist or a toxicologist to provide these antidotes. You have the means always at your own command. You have the recipe within yourself. "Prove me now herewith, saith the Lord of Hosts."

When you have learned how to use the law of counter suggestion, you can instantly neutralize the shock of an approaching storm, dissipate the bad effects of impending trouble and insulate yourself against violent reactions. You can do it by the simple method of displacing evil with good. Just as oil and water cannot mix, so mutually antagonistic thoughts cannot dwell together. The good always excludes the bad, and vice versa. You empty by filling.

One of the greatest problems encountered in perfecting radio reception was the elimination of static. One of the greatest problems in keeping the individual life in balance is to counteract the destructive thought currents and harmful suggestions which constantly knock at our doors, and, by the same token, constantly bring much unhappiness, sickness and suffering into our lives.

The practical Christian has solved this problem through the grace and strength of a poised mind. He has learned to live with his problems by living outside them. He has learned how to nullify conflicts and discords by refusing them entrance to his mind. By applying the right thought current to the wrong one, he has, as far as his individual life is concerned, stripped evil of its power.

YOUR BIGGEST PROBLEM

Your biggest problem as a Truth student is not: "How shall I heal my infirmities?" "How shall I increase my income?" "How shall I straighten out the difficulties in my home?" "How shall I attract more and better friends?" "How shall I become a great success?" "How shall I improve my environment?"

Your biggest problem is: "How shall I harmonize my mind with God's mind?" "How shall I conform my desires, my thoughts, my words and my acts with the principles of Truth?" "How shall I avoid mental conflicts and keep out of my mind the thoughts and combination of thoughts which make for conflict?" "How shall I avoid those greatest enemies to my success, inferiority, doubt, and discouragement?" These are the main problems, and upon their solution depends the solution of all the others.

There is a story by Hugh Walpole in which the hero buys a beautiful blue plate from a china shop. He takes the plate home and places it upon the mantel, and then sits down to glory in its beauty. But as he gazes at the lovely thing, he becomes aware that the house furnishings are not in harmony with the colorful plate. So he concludes that he must either give up the plate or refurnish the room. New pictures are hung, the wall colors are changed, the floor coverings replaced and the furniture reupholstered. Finally what began with a simple blue plate becomes a reharmonized and beautiful room, instead of a drab and commonplace one.

This story holds a real lesson for every seeker after the Kingdom of Heaven. For when we accept and embody its principles, Heaven becomes our mental "blue plate," leading us from self to God. It reminds us of Ernest in Hawthorne's story "The Great Stone Face." As a child he listened to the legend that some day there would come a great man to be the savior and leader of the people, who would resemble the face formed in the rock of the mountain. This massive, benevolent face of stone became a symbol to Ernest as he grew up beneath its shadow and went about his simple life, longing and waiting for the great man's coming.

But at the climax of the story the villagers suddenly realize that it is Ernest who resembles the great stone face. "So wholeheartedly did he believe the legend, so earnestly did he long for its fulfillment, and so constantly did his eyes dwell on the prophetic profile, that unconsciously his own features changed until, outwardly as well as inwardly; be completely embodied the ideal which his mind had absorbed ."

GET AN IDEAL

Jesus saw humanity groping in the dark, saw men beating out their lives with ungoverned passions, and destroying themselves with fears, worries, angers, resentments and hates. He saw us living in hell through divided minds, suffering because of ignorance, tormented by divided loyalties, tortured by unbalanced virtues and dying because of misunderstandings. He also saw the need of a new ideal, an ideal so powerful that it would transform everyone who embodied it in his thought.

Do you know what that ideal was? It was the Kingdom of Heaven as a present fact; not something imposed by God from the outside but something inherent in man. "Seek this Kingdom," He said. Put it first, and all these other things shall be added unto you. Then He proceeded to locate this Kingdom for them. "Neither shall they say, Lo, here, or Lo there" that is, not in some far off future world nor in the sky. "The Kingdom of God is within you."

The Kingdom of God has no geological location but is more like an imaginary line running through a man's life. It represents his "par life." Living on the upper side of that line he attracts blessings, and living on the lower side he attracts curses. The Kingdom's laws are self-acting. They work for us or against us according as we are obedient or disobedient to them. Then where does hell come in? It doesn't come in. It represents a distinct line of thinking by itself. Proceeding from the lower side of "par life," it is thinking, without God. It is there by virtue of living and thinking below par.

Do these two lines then ever meet? They do not. The only way you can ever get from one parallel to another is by turning and crossing over to if. When Jesus said that "The Kingdom of God is within you," He was talking not to the disciples, but to the Pharisees, who were "unregenerate people." "Is the Kingdom of God, then, in us all, God-centered and self-centered?" It most certainly is.

"Then what is the difference between God-centered and self-centered?" The God-centered are those who have embodied the Kingdom, live in it and enjoy its blessings; while the self-centered are those who live at cross purposes with it. The Kingdom of God is within them, too, but since they are unaware of It, It cannot function in their lives. It cannot operate for them.

St. Paul's statement that "Our citizenship is in Heaven" means that we cannot be citizens of two places, or states of consciousness, at one time, any more than we can be citizens of two countries at the same time. When a foreigner desires to receive citizenship in America, he must declare his intention, file his papers and renounce the government of his native land. He then ceases t o be an alien and becomes a citizen. Having renounced the laws of his native land, he is now under the laws of America.

GIVE UP SELF-MANAGEMENT

When Jesus told us to "Seek first the Kingdom of God and His righteousness," He meant that we were to give up self-management and to place ourselves under the law of God. This does not mean sacrificing our freedom, but losing our bondage. "And the government [of your life] shall be upon His shoulder." In entering the Kingdom of God we must do the same thing that the foreigner does when he adopts the citizenship of another country. "If ye be in Christ Jesus, ye are above the law and not subject to it."

When we renounce the dominion of the outer world and place ourselves under the righteous sovereignty of God, then we are no longer subject to the laws of the outer world but we are above them. Having renounced the laws of the flesh, we are now subject to the laws of Spirit. We are alien to evil and subject to God. We have put off the old man, and put on the new man, which is Christ.

Yes, our citizenship is in Heaven, but we have put ourselves in the impossible position of trying to be citizens of two countries at one and the same time. We want the blessings of Heaven but our ways of thinking and living indicate clearly that we still are loyal subjects of the outer world, still subject to appearances, still slaves to evil suggestions, still victims of irritations, fears, worries, jealousies and dislikes, rather than of the invisible Kingdom of Good within.

Jesus said: "No man can serve two masters." Neither can he live in two countries or in two states of mind at the same time. "Ye cannot serve God and mammon" (outer things and conditions which man has given power).

Jesus said in effect: "Therefore I charge you, be not anxious for your life, what ye shall eat, or what ye shall drink; nor about your body, what ye shall put on." "Be not therefore anxious saying, what shall we eat? or what shall we drink? or wherewithal shall we be clothed? For after all these things do the Gentiles seek: for your Heavenly Father knoweth that ye have need of all these things. But seek ye first His Kingdom [divine management — Government under God], and His righteousness; and all these things shall be added unto you."

In other words, you have only to place yourself under Divine management (harmonize your mind with His Mind), to "Let this mind be in you, which was also in Christ Jesus." Then your thinking and affairs will be according to His perfect plan. When you have the consciousness and realization of the Presence of God as being everywhere equally present, then you have the Mind of Christ and you are in Heaven. "And no man hath ascended up to Heaven, but He that came down from Heaven, even the son of man which is in Heaven."

"Only that can return to Heaven which was born in Heaven, and since Heaven is not a place, but a state of consciousness, the return must be a recognition that Heaven is already within. The son of man, who is also the Son of God, is already in Heaven and knows it not."

We said that the biggest problem in human life was not the solving of our problems or the healing of our ills, but the harmonizing of our minds with God's Mind. There are two steps in achieving this. First, we must have an ideal, and, second, we must make a place for it and provide for its growth. The ideal, of course, is the Kingdom of God within us (that to which all other things are added), and we make a place for it by surrendering from our minds everything that is unlike God or inimical to His Good, and by contemplating and embodying it within ourselves.

"TRANSFORMED INTO THE SAME IMAGE"

"We all ... beholding ... the glory of the Lord, are transformed into the same image." "What thou seest that thou beest." Whatever we are closely associated with in spirit and soul, dwell upon, contemplate—whatever is dominant in our thoughts will manifest itself in our flesh and in our affairs. To inwardly know the Presence of God is to find the Presence of God in every place, person, situation and thing.

Through intimacy of association, we are transformed into the same image. Beholding we are quickened. Looking we are changed. Steel kept in contact with a magnet soon becomes magnetized. Fabrics immersed in dye take on the color of the dye. Iron thrust into a furnace takes on the glow of the heat. Minds raised to God take on the Love and Power of God. When we enter Into Him, He enters into us.

"The contemplation of perfection is always uplifting." Nothing so clarifies the vision, enlarges the man, widens the consciousness as the determined and unceasing effort to measure up to one's ideal. "The struggle to better our best, to make our highest moments permanent, the continual reaching of the mind for the things above and beyond, the steady pursuit of the ideal, which constantly advances as we pursue, is what has led the race up from savagery to twentieth century civilization."

Without an ideal, on the other hand, there is no advancement, and where there is no advancement there is retrogression. "Where there is no vision," says the writer of Proverbs, "the people perish." The universe is not static but dynamic. Everything moves. Nothing stands still. Where people do not move forward they move backward. Everything in a man's life depends upon the direction in which he faces and the direction depends upon his ideals. It is upward or downward, backward or forward for every man.

Jesus said: "I go to prepare a place for you, that where I am, there ye may be also." When God made man He also made a house for him to live in. The Kingdom of God was stamped into the structure of every man's being from the beginning. It was the place and way in which he was intended to live. "And God said, Let us make man in our image; after our likeness:

and let them have DOMINION." This means that if we live according to the Image (keep God foremost in our thought) we shall have dominion, and if we do not live according to It we shall have bondage.

"Your circumstances may be uncongenial," says James Allen, "but they shall not long remain so if you but perceive an ideal and strive to reach it. You cannot grow within and stagnate without. If you follow the line that runs parallel with your good; if you obey the urge which says 'Come up higher, If you listen to the voice which bids you to arise, to look up, to think up, to lift up, then no matter how distressing your outer circumstances may seem, your life will be a crowning success."

Bishop Phillip Brooks said: "The ideal life of full completion haunts us all. We feel the thing we ought to be beating beneath the thing we are. God hides some ideal in every human soul. At some time in his life, each feels a trembling, fearful longing to do some great good thing. Life finds its noblest spring of excellence in its hidden impulse to do one's best."

THE INVOLUNTARY PRINCIPLE OF LIVING

The power and ability of a leader is determined not by the number of things he does by and for himself, but by the number of things he gets others to do for him. The ideal principle of living as outlined by Jesus is the involuntary principle. "Of mine own self," He said, "I can do nothing. The Father within, He doeth the works." "Consider the lilies of the field, HOW they grow. They toil not, neither do they spin. Behold, the fowls of the air: they sow not nor gather into barns, and yet your Heavenly Father feedeth them," etc., etc.

It is natural for those who have the authority or means to want others to manage as much of their lives as they can delegate to them. The business man wants business managers, assistants, salesmen, contact men, secretaries, bookkeepers, stenographers and errand boys. The general must have colonels, majors, captains and lieutenants . The lieutenant must have sergeants, corporals and privates. The house wife must have maids and cooks, chauffeurs and gardeners. But there are other things (invisible things) which no one can manage for us but God. For these things we must have management at the top.

When Jesus told us to give up self-management by putting God first in our lives, He meant that we were to give up all negative thoughts, destructive attitudes, preconceived opinions, race consciousness, false beliefs and false reactions to whatever may be happening in our world.

"Leave all and follow me" means to give up the sense of personal responsibility, doubts, fears, worries, quandaries, the feeling of haste and the pressure of time. To give up disappointments, anxieties, perplexities, prejudices and adverse thoughts. To give up our feelings of despair, futility and frustration. To surrender our antagonisms, grievances, grudges and emotions. To surrender our limitations, weaknesses, illnesses and disabilities.

GIVE GOD FIRST PLACE

"I the Lord thy God am a jealous God." "Thou shalt have no other gods before me." This does not mean that God is jealous in the sense that one person is jealous of another, but that He demands the first and supreme place in our lives. "I am God and beside me there is none else." He is jealous only in the sense that He demands access to every area of our lives. "Look unto me" means to put God first in every problem. "Call upon me in the day of trouble and I will deliver thee." That is the only demand that God makes upon us — that we recognize Him and give Him first place in our thought.

But how can we do this when our thought is taken up with so many things that are unlike God? How can the Almighty work in our behalf when He cannot even get into our minds? We may not like the situations in which we find ourselves but there certainly is no way out until we surrender our thoughts and feelings concerning them, and put God in their stead.

"Look unto me": Stop trying to see your own way. "Come unto me": Stop trying to solve problems and meet difficulties in your own strength. "Trust me"! Stop looking to others for your good and look to the Father within. "Lean on me": Stop leaning on your own wisdom and ask of God. Put first things first. Put God where your trouble seems to be and trouble will flee. Demonstrate principles and not things.

"I will walk in you and talk in you." Let God have His way in you and He will give you the best there is. Let God have your body and He will fill it with health. Let God have your mind and He will fill it with power. Let God have your life and He will fill it with riches. You do not need to find God; let Him find you. Clear a space for Him. Do it many times a day. Do it when the going is rough and do it when things are going well. Put Him first in everything.

If destructive thoughts are standing in the way of your good then blast them out. Bomb them out. Put pressure on the subconscious mind to let go. Give Him no rest until He establishes it. "Make a place for God." It is better to light a candle than to curse the darkness. Let your light shine. Make it take the place of darkness. The Divine Presence is like the air. It will automatically find any place that you make for it.

GET A SENSE OF DOMINION

"And God said, 'Let us make man in our image, after our likeness and let them have dominion'." The way to get dominion over the circumstance—the world, is to be dominated by God, to put Him first in every situation and in every need. But "How do I get this sense of dominion?" you ask. By practicing the Presence of God. Yes, I know that sounds mystical and vague, but let Jan Debonheur clarify it for us:

"As you have heard many times before, mind acts under its own conception of itself. Now if I conceive myself as being just John Doe, with the usual limitations and perhaps a few more, what reason have I for thinking that my word has power? I have always seemed to be powerless, haven't I? But if I conceive myself to be the expression, or 'pressing out,' of God; if I realize that 'I and the Father are one' and that 'With God all things are possible,' then, because of what I conceive myself to be, and because mind acts under its own conception of itself—my word goes forth with power and I know that I have but to speak it and it is done.

"John Doe has no power, but 'With God all things are possible.' As a son of God and an individualization of Infinite Mind, you have the authority and power to dominate and control your circumstances, and you do this through your consciousness of oneness with the Father."

Now what is that great demonstration you are trying to make, or that great obstacle you are trying to overcome? Is it something you want to acquire, or something you want to get rid of? You must be sure that you know, and you must definitely formulate your idea of what you want, and then speak the word with authority.

In every demonstration there always are two parts—God's part and your part. Your part is to create the pattern, to have understanding and faith, and God's part is to fill the pattern you have made. "The Kingdom of God is within you" means that the good you are seeking is in the center of your being, ready to spring into manifestation when you ask believing. "There is a spirit in man." You have only to recognize the Divine Spirit within you and within your problem, and name what you want in order to bring it forth as an actual manifestation in your outer world.

"The word of God is instant, and powerful, and it always works." This means that when your faith in God is strong enough to connect your consciousness with His consciousness, then the action will be instantaneous. Your good will spring forth speedily. Delayed results, on the other hand, should not discourage you in your efforts to demonstrate. Instant action comes out of sustained thinking, and that comes only through long practice and meditation.

Let us begin, then, by starting each day with a clear understanding of God's place in our affairs. Let us contemplate the statement that follows, and meditate upon it until there no longer are any problems in our lives:

"Today God is my partner, and He is leading me. I look to Him for direction in all my affairs. I will be a simple

follower today. God will be everywhere I am. My Good will be everywhere I am.

"God continually welcomes me into His Presence. I shall be received gladly wherever I go; for I go by the direct call of God.

"My whole life today is being run by the Father. Every word that I speak is God-inspired, and will bring God inspired results.

"Because God is my partner today, I shall not be in want of any good thing—health, courage, strength, faith, stamina, supply, harmony or ideas. Divine Wisdom uses me today as a perfect instrument through which to express itself.

"This day will be the happiest, the fullest, the most productive of good of any I have ever experienced. Amen."

IV
"Thy Kingdom Come" in My Problems

"Elijah arose, and did eat and drink, and went in the strength of that meat for forty days and forty nights unto Horeb the mount of God."

"The old Latin proverb SOLVITUR AMBULANDO means 'The problem is solved by walking,' or by action. It always helps, when one is depressed or burdened by events, to get up or go out and do something.

"But while any kind of action may relieve the pressure of a problem, not any kind of action will help to solve it. Going away for a time to escape creditors is action, but it solves nothing. Doing something just to make me forget my trouble, may help me to forget it for the moment: but I haven't thereby mastered it, or transformed it. Action of this sort is only self-deception: it is not what the proverb means.

"The action that is of value, is that which has in it the promise of leading us both out of ourselves and on to a new vantage ground from which we can see further than we could see before, and also see the past in better perspective something also which will give us a better hold upon ourselves, because it gives us a better hold on reality, on God.

"Elijah's action was significant in this respect. He ran away from Jezebel through fear; but later his reason for going to Mount Horeb was to get a new hold upon God, and so upon himself. This was the right kind of action."

In his book THE STAR OF LIFE, Dr. V. P. Randall says that if we examine our problems, "be they of morals, mind, body or business we discover that in the last analysis they are problems of lack, want, limitation, poverty. Something is lacking which if it were the problem would not be there." Always this is true.

We readily recognize that poverty is lack of money, but back of the lack of money is a consciousness of limitation or an impoverished mind. Fear, which plays such a devastating role in human affairs, is lack of faith, courage and confidence in God. Disease in all its many ramifications is an impoverished condition arising from negative thinking and a lack of strength, health or vitality. "Sorrow is a dark shadow which is cast over us when the positive qualities of joy, happiness and other related states of mind are shut out. It is that which man drops back into when the supporting strength of Joy has been taken away.

"So with every problem of human life. Not one could exist without there first had been taken away, shut out or otherwise prevented from expressing itself in man, some positive, true, real quality — some quality or attribute of God, some essential element of His Holy Spirit."

"Therefore, as we enter this chapter on problems, we shall keep two things before us. First, we shall be obedient to the words of St. Paul in his epistle to the Romans: 'Be not overcome of evil, but overcome evil with good.' And, second, we shall cease to think of destroying, but rather think of creating; we shall be concerned not with losing, but with finding. We shall think of overcoming in terms of laying hold upon Reality and Truth — the Reality and Truth of God in all its Sufficiency and Abundance of all the good of every sort that our lives can ever need."

THE PROBLEM OF SICKNESS

If your problem is one of sickness, then be still and know that the Spirit in the center of your being is the spirit of perfect health. Clear a space in your body for this perfect health. Make room in your consciousness for it. Put the thought of sickness out of your mind for the moment and speak health into activity. It is there now awaiting your recognition. "We all . . . beholding . . . the glory of the Lord, are transformed into the same image."

Through recognition the miracle happens. Through realization the Divine Current is released. Through acceptance the body is quickened. "Speak the word only, and my servant shall be healed." MY BODY IS GOD'S TEMPLE, WHOLE, STRONG, PERFECT AND FREE. Put this thought where the sickness seemed to be. Feel God's mighty healing power surging through your entire being, vitalizing, strengthening, rebuilding and making you every whit whole. "And God said, 'Let the dry land appear'." The impossible is about to take place. Health out of sickness. Strength out of weakness. "Dry land out of wet water."

The Divine Current released through your spoken word quickens the radiation of health. The health within responds immediately to the spoken word of faith and begins instantly to restore health to every organ and function of the body, and you are made whole.

RIGHT WORK

If your problem is one of vocational guidance or obtaining the right position, then take the matter to God. "If any man lack wisdom, let him ask of God, Who giveth to all men liberally, and upbraideth not." If you have gotten from your present position all that it has for you in the way of experience, training, discipline and patience, then affirm that God, Who is everywhere equally present, knows what your right work is, where it is, and that God is leading you to it and it to you. "Ask ... believing." Make your declaration clear and positive. Be definite.

"God in me knows what my right work is, where it is, and exactly what I ought to do to be actually engaged in it."

Make your statement with determination, conviction and firmness. Use it many times a day, but do not allow it to become a mere mechanical repetition of words. Know that what you affirm is the absolute Truth. IT IS TRUE NOW. Feel it so deeply that you impress it upon the subconscious mind, where all creation takes place. Give life to your affirmation through sustained thinking. Give spirit to it through your faith. Give power to it through your acceptance. Then say:

"Let this knowledge be quickened (made active and alive) in me as a revelation to my conscious mind, so I shall know, and know that I know, what Is my right work, where it is, and what there is for me to do to become established in it."

So it is with every other need in your life, whether it be adjustment, guidance, healing, supply, harmony, peace, success or what you will. "Ask whatsoever ye will (nothing excluded), and it shall be done unto you." By putting God in the place where your need seems to be, and naming the thing you want, you speak into instant action the thing that is already yours. Please notice that the term used so many times in this section of the book, "Putting God in the place where your need seems to be," means literally to keep God in the center of your consciousness.

THE DISAGREEABLE PERSON

Is there some one in your life whom you do not like, who rubs you the wrong way, who, as you say, gets on your nerves, and whose point of view and whose behavior you cannot stand? Is it impossible for you to love this person, to work with him, to get along with him, to agree with him? Then stop trying. Do not even attempt to visualize him as God's child. If you have tried and failed to harmonize yourself with him, then turn him over to God.

Put this person out of your consciousness by refusing to think of him, and put God in his place. Black his personality out by flooding God's Presence in. Just say to yourself. "This is a good spot to make room for God." Then let go. Give un all your ideas, attitudes, beliefs, thoughts and emotions concerning him.

Instead of thinking of the person and his shortcomings and errors, think of God and keep thinking of Him until the offending personality fades from your mind. That is all you have to do. Keep God in the center of your consciousness and He will do the rest.

FAULTFINDING AND CRITICISM

Are you given to faultfinding and criticism? Do you find so much lack in others that it is beginning to manifest itself in you and your affairs? Then do not let another hour go by without doing something about it. Apply the antidote. Make a place for God. When the impulse to criticise or condemn someone or something comes to you, refuse to express it. Say instead, "Here is a good place to make room for God." Instead of stinging or lashing the object of your condemnation, look closely to see if there is not something good in it to praise. Can you see this good?

Can you let the Real in you call to the Real in others, or in things? If you can't, then you can at least put the seal of silence on your lips and say nothing. But you must not stop there.

As St. Paul says, "A little leaven leaveneth the whole lump." There are few if any circumstances in which you cannot see some good. Since God is everywhere, then Good must be everywhere. Good is in every person, place, situation and thing, and if you cannot see it, then it is because you have allowed the worst to impress you. Good is in the one you criticise because God is there. '"A little leaven leaveneth the whole lump."

If you would break this vicious habit and fill your life with beauty, then you must find the good in all that you formerly condemned and call it forth. Instead of criticising and condemning, use praise and blessing. Instead of looking for the worst, look for the best. Instead of magnifying the evil magnify the good. Make a place for God. When the impulse to find fault, to criticise and condemn comes to you, refuse to express it. Say instead: "FOR THE GOOD THAT IS IN YOU, I PRAISE YOU AND PRAISE YOU AND BLESS YOU."

THE GRUDGE CARRIER

Are you a grudge carrier? Do you find it hard to forgive real or imaginary hurts? Do you spend precious time mentally hashing and rehashing the things that have happened to you, the things people have said about you, the injustices that have come to you? Are you filled with hatred, retaliation and revenge? If this is the sort of stuff that festers in your mind then you need to clean house. You need to make a place for God. "He makes darkness light before me, and crooked places straight."

Clean out the old grudges and fancied slights and put God in their place. Think of Him instead. Bury the hatchet and the venomous weapons of hatred, bitterness and revenge. When you have a retaliatory thought, a resentful or driven thought, an unloving thought, a "getting even" thought—if it is of a nature to unbalance you and fill you with poison— whatever it is, let go of it. Give it to God. Wipe it out of your consciousness.

Remind yourself that it is impossible to injure another willingly without injuring yourself in return.

Before Jesus' days in the flesh it was "An eye for an eye," hate for hate, bitterness for bitterness, revenge for revenge, injury for injury, blow for blow; but He taught that we must not retaliate, resist or strike back. "Ye have heard that it hath been said, An eye for an eye, and a tooth for a tooth but I say unto you, That ye resist not evil but whosoever shall smite thee on the right cheek, turn to him the other also."

"Ye have heard that it hath been said, Thou shalt love thy neighbor, and hate thine enemy. But I say unto you, Love your enemies, bless them that curse you, do good to them that hate you, and pray for them which despitefully use you, and persecute you."

This statement is as scientific as are the laws of gravitation and mathematics. For real or fancied slights we are to substitute love, blessing and prayer. Why? Because hatred and revenge only rob us of power and mar our achievements, while love, blessing and prayer keep us in touch with God and full of power.

To be good to ourselves, we must be good to others. To be emancipated from vicious thoughts, we must forgive everybody for everything at all times, and not only forgive but forget. True forgiveness includes forgetting. If you will only practice forgiveness every day and especially before you go to sleep at night, forgiving everybody and yourself as well, you will stir up such power in yourself as you have never felt before.

FEAR OF INHERITED TRAITS

Is your problem the fear of inherited traits, tendencies and diseases? Do you carry in your mind a belief that some terrible disease runs in your family — that you inherited deafness from an uncle, bad eyesight from your mother and stomach trouble from your father; that you have to be careful about your lungs because a brother died of tuberculosis? If any of these bogies float around in your consciousness, then indeed you must put God in their place.

You do not have to go into great detail in such things, telling Him what all these potential ailments and fears are, nor how they came into your mind, but just to be aware of His Presence, His willingness and His transcendent power to blot them out of your life.

When you stop giving your attention (thought energy) to them and put God in their place, then you will be healed. He will blot them out forever. Can you aid in this process? You certainly can. Every time a belief or thought of this kind presents itself to you, turn upon it and declare: "GOD IS MY FATHER. FROM HIM I INHERIT GOOD, ALL GOOD AND ONLY GOOD."

INFERIORITY

It is safe to say that if all the blighted ambitions, all the stunted lives and all the human failures were stacked together in one pile and analyzed, it would be found that the underlying cause of most of these casualties was inferiority, doubt or despair. Inferiority is the great curse of the human race; it does more to hold people down and keep them from doing what they could do than almost any other one thing. It is man at his lowest ebb in subordination and weakness.

Inferiority is living in the consciousness of limitation and defeat, and in the satisfaction of little things. It is resignation to the defective, deficient, little man, unable to rise above his environment instead of cultivating the grander more glorious man which everyone is capable of becoming. Jesus said: "Be ye therefore perfect, even as your Father which is in Heaven is perfect."

But how can one be perfect who constantly thinks imperfect thoughts? How can one be whole who is forever talking about his deficiencies and shortcomings? How can one rise to prominence who thinks he was made for little things, who constantly rehearses his limitations and inhibitions? How can one rise to perfection when he inwardly believes that there is something seriously wrong with him? How can one expect to overcome his difficulties, solve his problems and heal his diseases if he cannot get beyond himself?

St. Paul said: "Put off the old man and put on the new man, which is Christ." Put off this miserable, weak, inefficient, inferior man who has been masquerading as your real self, and put on the grander man you long to be, the victorious man you can be, the perfect man you will be.

Are you tired of a narrow, humdrum, cheap existence? Are you tired of being ordinary, surrounded with ordinary things? Are you tired of being mediocre, filling mediocre jobs and working with mediocre people? Are you tired of thwarted ambitions, unanswered prayers and unfilled desires? Are you tired of being unable to do the things you want to do? Then why tolerate this inferior self any longer? Why let him mess up your life any further? Why not put him where he belongs, in the limbo of forgotten things?

Why not call out the greater, superior man who is equal to every need? Why not let him live in you, think for you and act for you? Why not let him build a new reputation for you, a new body, new circumstances, new conditions? Is it because you do not know how to do it? Then it is very simple. All you have to do is to keep out of your mind everything that you do not want expressed in your life, and keep in your mind everything you want expressed.

If you want something better than what you now possess, put yourself in the positive affirmative attitude that can draw it to you. Change your wave length. Get into tune with God. Ask Him to nerve you with incessant affirmatives. Don't magnify that which you lack. Chant the beauties of the Good. Refuse to express a limitation and it dies. When Alexander Dumas was threatened with the curse of race inferiority he said: "When I found that I was black, I resolved to live as if I were white and so force men to look below my skin."

Robert A. Russell

It makes no difference what your prospects or opportunities may be, nor how much education or ability you may have, if you are held in leash by an ingrained conviction that you are inferior to others, to your ambitions, to your dreams, to your ideals, to your aspirations, to the man you long to be, to the position you long to hold, to the place you long to fill; if you are holding in mind suggestions of limitation, weakness and mediocrity; if you have a low estimate of yourself; if you think meanly of yourself; if you do not believe in yourself; if you carry the impression that you cannot do what you want to do, that you haven't the ability, that you lack the brain power.

If you are visualizing a little defective, inferior creature, then no matter what you do, nor how hard you try, nor how much you may pray, you are bound to be a miserable failure. You will fail, not because you are unable to accomplish what you set out to do, but because your mind is saturated with your own inferiority.

Is there a cure for such a malady? There certainly is. "Greater is he that is in you than he that is in the world." "Put ye on the Lord Jesus Christ." You can cure yourself by changing the mental model you are holding of yourself. "Now are we the sons of God," said St. John, "and it doth not yet appear what we shall be: but we know that, when He shall appear, we shall be like Him."

"There is a Christ in you" (the Perfect Model of every man) which is superior to every problem, circumstance and condition in your life. He is your "hope of glory," as Rt. Paul said, — the man you could have been, the man you can be now, "the man God intended you to be." He is your Real Self, your neglected self, the Greater man you are capable of becoming.

He is even now standing at the door of your consciousness, knocking for your recognition and awaiting your acceptance.

If you will open the door and release Him into expression from the Great Within of yourself; if you will contemplate Him by seeing yourself as God intended you to be, the man you want to be and can be; if you will see yourself in perfection as God made you; if you will hold yourself in thought without handicap, limitation, defect, or blemish; if you will constantly see yourself as the larger, invincible, dauntless and fearless man God created and never lose sight of Him, then you will rise superior to every problem, circumstance and unfriendly person in your world.

You will be equal to every need and rise victorious over every condition; over everything that keeps you from your Good. The perfect things will gravitate toward you and the imperfect things will fall away. By holding to a higher and more perfect ideal of yourself you will rise to higher and higher standards.

"Be ye therefore perfect, even as your Father which is in Heaven is perfect." The way to make yourself perfect is to think yourself into perfection by the contemplation and embodiment of perfect thoughts. If you would awake in His likeness, then you must live in His Consciousness. Admit no limitation. Accept no deficiency. Hold no fear. Think of yourself as you are in God, as you want to be, ought to be and can be. Hold a better opinion of yourself. Think more of yourself. If God is good and you are made in His image and likeness, then you must be good, too.

Stop squandering God's possibilities. Stop visualizing a cheap success. If you are God's son then the best is none too good for you. Stop stifling your aspirations. Stop holding a low estimate of yourself. Be true to your ideal. Don't let anybody tell you that you cannot do what you want to do, that you cannot be what you want to be. Nurse your goals and feed your visions. Follow the star and you will arrive. If you would do the biggest thing possible for you, then stop being John Doe, and be Christ.

"I can do all things through Christ which strengtheneth me." "Through Christ" means through cooperation with the inner man. If you are made in God's image as the Bible states, then you can never be inferior. Hold the perfect model in your mind and live up to it. If there is inferiority in your mind, then it is because you put it there. You can overcome it by keeping your mind off self and on God. By keeping in mind the things you want to bring about in your life, and by keeping out of mind the things you do not want, every needed adjustment will be made.

Jesus said, "If ye abide in me, ask what ye will, and it shall be done unto you." Abiding in God brings improvement in your affairs, while abiding in self brings deterioration.

DOUBT

Another insidious foe to human success is doubt. Like inferiority, it is a barrier to most anything one sets out to do. "Our doubts are traitors," said Shakespeare, "and make us lose the good we oft might win by fearing to attempt." Doubt is not only the most prolific source of human frustration and defeat, but the greatest barrier to healing and all worthy achievement.

"Are you sure that you are doing the right thing?" "Wouldn't it be better to wait until another time?" "Do you really think you can do it?" "Do you think you had better take a chance?" "Did you go into the matter thoroughly?" "Did you take this into consideration?" "Did you hear what so and so said?" These and a thousand other questions will not only sap the vigor of a man's ambitions, but will, if he listens to them and acts upon them, destroy his initiative and keep him from accomplishing anything worth while.

"A double-minded man," says St. James, "is unstable in all his ways. Let not that man think that he shall receive anything of the Lord." The doubters are the procrastinators, the vacillators, the misgivers, the deliberators, the hesitators, the pettifoggers, the floaters and the drifters. They never can get anywhere because they are influenced by every wind that blows. They are always waiting for a more propitious season, during which period of hesitation the self-confident man claims all the prizes.

They receive nothing because they lack confidence in themselves and in their ability to accomplish what they would like to do. They hesitate and waver because they have no definite goal. They are undecided as to which way to turn.

"Nine men out of every ten," says Dr. William Mathews, "lay out their plans on too vast a scale and they who are competent to do almost anything do nothing, because they never make up their minds distinctly as to what they want, or what they intend to be. Hence the mournful failures we see all around us in every walk of life."

Doubt says: "Wait a minute. Take plenty of time. Let someone else take the risk. You'll get a better break later on. Don't be in a hurry. There's too much opposition. You are sticking your neck out. You haven't a ghost of a show. You haven't the capital. You haven't the pull. There are too many obstacles in the way. There is too much competition. The odds are against you. No one else has been able to do it," etc., etc., and then the thing you hoped to do und felt you could do is never begun.

You hesitated so long that you lost your courage, your resolution, your tenacity and your grit. By talking it over with others you talked it out of your life.

"The man who is perpetually hesitating which of two things he will do first," says William Wirt, "will do neither. The man who resolves, but suffers his resolution to be changed by the first counter suggestion of a friend—who fluctuates from opinion to opinion, from plan to plan, and veers like a weathercock to every point of the compass, with every breath of caprice that blows; can never accomplish anything great or useful. Instead of being progressive in anything, he will at best be stationary, and, more probably, retrograde in all.

"It is only the man who carries into his life pursuits that great quality which Lucan ascribes to Caesar, 'nescia virtus stare loco'—who first consults wisely, and then executes his purpose with inflexible perseverance, undismayed by those petty difficulties which daunt a weaker spirit—that can advance to eminence in any line."

If you were to analyze your doubts carefully you would find that, on the whole, they stem from a sense of your own responsibility, and that is why you do not do what the inner man tells you you can do. The antidote, of course, is self-confidence, and the cure is to change your position in the Law—to realize that you are dealing with Law and not personality. You can accomplish whatever you want to do, achieve anything you want to achieve, IF you know that it is God Who is doing it, and not you. As St. James said you must "ask in faith, NOTHING DOUBTING. For he that wavereth is like a wave of the sea driven with the wind and tossed."

Never say, therefore, that you are not good enough to heal, or that you do not know enough, or that you do not understand enough. Jesus said: "What the Son seeth the Father do these also doeth the Son in like manner." Know that you are dealing with the Law and regard all limiting suggestions as lies; shut the door on them and refuse to entertain them. Know that Truth works independently and demonstrates itself. The only doubt that is fatal is that doubt which you retain and feed.

But suppose you are not able to bring yourself to a point of conviction about the thing you are affirming. How will you crystallize the belief in your mind? How will you give it form and power? By firm and repeated repetition of the affirmation (revolving it in your mind) until the subjective state of your thought accepts it as true. First, get a clear picture of what you want to do, or the thing you want to bring into your experience, and then make up your mind to accomplish it (tie it up in your consciousness by acceptance), not by yourself but through the Law.

Weigh the facts carefully, consider every angle thoroughly, and, then act accordingly. Keep repeating your affirmation in deep faith and acceptance until all trace of doubt is gone. Abide in it, dwell on it, meditate upon it, live with it, breathe it, sleep with it work with it, until you have induced within your consciousness a definite acceptance of an already established fact. Hold the positive, creative attitude and know that your good will be objectified at that point in mind where your doubt disappears. Know that you are going to succeed.

Praise the Lord. Bless the good that is within you. Fill your mind with bright, optimistic, happy pictures. Foresee a glorious, overwhelming success in everything you undertake. Thank God for the success that is coming toward you. Expect the best and look for the best. Stop criticising. Stop finding fault and stop condemning yourself and others. Plan for big things and make quick decisions. Place no limitation on anything or anybody.

When Alexander was asked how he had conquered the world, he replied that he did it by not delaying. And you will conquer your world by the same principle. "Be wise today; 'tis madness to defer."

Metaphysicians have many theories on the first step in making a demonstration, but let us take our authority from the scriptures as contained in St. Mark's Gospel, 11th chapter, 23rd verse: "For verily I say unto you, That whosoever shall say unto this mountain, Be thou removed, and be thou east into the sea; and shall not doubt in his heart, but shall believe that those things which he saith shall come to pass; he shall have whatsoever he saith."

Isn't it obvious that if there were no doubts there would be no need to affirm, to treat or to pray for things; and also that where doubt continues there is a definite barrier to healing and answered prayer?

Then what is the first step in demonstration? To remove doubt, of course. And how will you do that? By having nothing to do With It. By unfolding out of it. Since doubt is nothing but a thought saying that you cannot do this or that other thing, then only a thought of an opposite nature can unsay it. Declare:

"My word is the Law unto that thing whereunto it is spoken, and it will be become fulfilled in the right way and at the right time, and all doubt will disappear."

Never say: ·"I wish I could do thus and so?" or, "I don't believe I can." Carry the victorious attitude. Say:

"As I let fall the forms of my thought they are acted upon by Principles I believe. This is the Law of God, the Law of man, and the Law of the Universe."

Never say: "If it be Thy Will"; but rather, "THY WILL BE DONE."

Then recognize that the Divine Will is always the best that you can conceive for yourself or anybody else. Be sure of yourself and doubt can get no hold upon your life. Be confident. Be faithful. If it is in accord with the Law of God, never give up the thing you have set your heart upon. Never hesitate to attempt the unusual.

When you are working with God, never think of yourself as presumptuous in attempting the seemingly impossible. Never put off till tomorrow what you want to do today. Be superior to fluctuation. Laugh at opposition. See yourself as larger than your calling. Be impervious to contempt and ridicule. Then the Universe will not only listen to what you have to say, but it will lay its treasures at your feet.

DISCOURAGEMENT

There probably is no other one thing except worry so depressing to the body and mind as discouragement.

Discouragement has thwarted more ambitions, destroyed more enthusiasm, stunted more careers, injured more lives, starved more souls, ruined more hopes, wasted more energy, killed more incentive, paralyzed more effort and made more suicides than any other one thought. It. is a disease of the mind which attacks everyone in some form. Everyone is more or less injured by it. It invades us from the outside and from the inside, and when chronic spreads like a forest fire.

The person who says he is getting no better is hastening the end which he fears. The discouraged man is the beaten man. He is whipped before he starts. He is whipped because he has made his mind negative instead of positive, destructive instead of constructive. In other words, he has demoralized his whole being.

Now, stop and think of the damage you do every time you allow yourself to become discouraged. Think of the handicaps you place upon your life. Discouragement paralyzes your efficiency and takes away your resourcefulness, originality and enthusiasm. It so depresses your mental faculties and robs them of their power that there no longer is any coordination among them.

You have disqualified yourself, so to speak, by stopping your initiative and strangling your ability. You have crippled your mentality for the time being, and until this mood has been counteracted by the contemplation of its opposite (joyous expectancy of better things to come), you will be in the position toward life of the proverbial ship without a rudder.

Since success begins in the mind, every time you allow yourself to be discouraged; every time you belittle yourself; every time you give up; every time you stop trying; every time you give way to despondency; every time you allow yourself to be influenced by fear; every time you doubt your ability; every time you give in to hopelessness, you are turning away from God. You are driving from you the very blessings you want to demonstrate. You are ruining your possibilities by an attitude which is antagonistic to them.

You start on your adventure with high hopes, with great enthusiasm and courage — then some reverse, disappointment or setback comes and you begin to weaken. Then you wonder if you really are doing the right thing; if you are on the right track; if God is going to keep His promise, if you are equal to the task, etc., etc. The more power you give such thoughts the bigger they become. Your hope finally dwindles, and you give up. Your resolution is allowed to atrophy because things didn't work out as you had planned. Your faith in God, so strong in the beginning, now is nothing more than a myth.

What, then, is the remedy for this insidious disease? Turn yourself around mentally and cultivate that Mind from which you came. Emerson said: "What I need is somebody who will make me do what I can."

What the discouraged person needs is to be shown that he is not suffering from a condition or weakness over which he has no control, but from an idea operating through his mind, and that since the idea is mental it is under his control at all times.

Since most discouragement comes from within, from a lack of understanding and faith in oneself, then it must be controlled at its source. It must be controlled by saturating the mind with confidence and assurance of good things to come. The discouraged person must be forced to face the light, to change his thought and to alter his position in the Light. He must be taught to rely on his Higher Self at all times and stay away from failures, pessimists and all who do not believe in themselves.

"A man is known by the company he keeps." "Birds of a feather flock together." Tramps flock with tramps. Drinkers flock with drinkers. Successful men flock with other successful men. "It takes a thief to catch a thief." "Water seeks its own level." "Misery loves company." If therefore one would be strong, he must seek the company of those in a consciousness higher than his own. He must not "associate with weak people, weak thoughts and weak motives."

The word discouragement means literally to be separated from courage-from God. It means discontinuance of the power to achieve, to succeed. It is a belief that we are standing alone, separated from God, with the consequent consciousness of weakness and impotence. It is that state wherein the salt hath lost its savor. Life then will be a succession of upsets, good or bad according to our reaction to these conditions.

We can cure this condition by reuniting ourselves with God, by focusing all our energies on strength and power. The discouraged person needs to be re-charged and re-tempered with Power from on High. He needs to recapture again that firmness of spirit which meets trouble and problems without fear. How does one do that? By clearing his mind of everything which stands between himself and God, and by giving free access to the flow of Divine Power.

What the discouraged person needs more than anything else is the consciousness that he is supported by a Power greater than his own, and that, in so far as he trusts in It and relies on It, It will rush to his assistance in every emergency and in every need.

The secret of all dominion and power is contained in an individual's ability to drive from his consciousness by an antidote against them every suggestion of doubt, fear, inferiority, failure, weakness, depression, disappointment, dismay and discouragement. The fact that two opposite thoughts cannot occupy the mind at the same time means that every man is the absolute master of himself at all times.

Paradoxical as it may seem, nothing ever happens to any of us except what happens through us. To be strong or weak, superior or inferior, prosperous or poor is a simple thing of choice. It all depends upon the thoughts we embody in our minds, upon whether our habitual thinking is centered in God or centered in self.

A PARABLE

There is a story about the mythical character commonly known as the devil that shows just how discouragement, which man sometimes thinks is the devil, works. As the story goes an old farmer traveling in strange lands came across an odd-looking building, unlike anything that he had ever seen. He found it to be a warehouse in which were kept the seeds of all the thoughts that spring up in man whenever he gets busy planting. There he found certain packets of seeds, one marked "malice," another "hatred," another "jealousy," another "deceit," another "sensuousness," another "hypocrisy," another "revenge." There was vice of every kind in those packets.

Apart from the rest was a pile very much larger than all the others, and, strange to say, it was marked "discouragement." While the farmer was wondering about this the devil came along; the farmer questioned him and said: "How is it that you have so much 'discouragement' here? I didn't know that belonged to you." The devil said: "Not many people know it belongs to me, and I don't mean them to. Most people pull these other weeds up at once. Not so with discouragement, for it will grow everywhere; it springs up so quickly and hides and conceals and keeps out of sight those other things, until they are strong enough to stand alone. And it is such a harmless looking weed that very few people suspect I have anything to do with it."

After this long speech of the devil's, the farmer thought a moment, then said: "You say discouragement will grow everywhere; will it really grow everywhere?"

"Well, no," said the devil; there is one place where I never could get discouragement to grow."

"Where is that?" asked the farmer.

"That," said the devil, "is in the heart of a man who trusts God."

In this little parable we have the secret of overcoming discouragement—the thought that we are inferior, that we have failed, that we are weak, deficient and defective; this thought that we are helpless and afraid, that everything is against us, that we cannot succeed, that we cannot do what we want to do.

Take God into your consciousness and you will have, not only the power to overcome all trials, troubles, disappointments and heartaches, but to fulfill every ambition to the letter. Then, in spite of all appearances to the contrary, in spite of the things that apparently are trying to hold you down, you will carry out your life plan victoriously and make manifest the mighty Power within you.

Say many times each day:

"I am strong and of good courage; I turn not to the right hand nor to the left.

"I am a child of the King of Kings and have nothing to fear. If I always do the best I can in all circumstances, there is no reason why I should ever be anxious about the results. I shall not.

"I am courage. I am success. Nothing can harm me because I am one with the One.

"I cannot want, I cannot fall, because I am in touch with the Infinite Source of all life."

V
Big Difficulties and Little Difficulties

"Wherefore take unto you the whole armor of God, that ye may be able to withstand in the evil day, and having done all, to stand."

The only difference between big difficulties and little ones is the measure of our spiritual strength, whether our faith in God is shallow or deep, our reserves high or low. Actually, as Emerson said, "There is no great and no small to the soul that maketh all." Big and little are just relative terms, like black and white, up and down, east and west, light and darkness.

Big and little problems, like incurable and curable diseases, are simply the results of our personal reactions to the things that happen to us — our way of viewing them. It is always the reaction that determines the result.

One problem seems bigger than another because our spiritual resistance is low, because we are not equal to it, not fortified against it, and because we view it through a frustrated and obstacle-possessed mind. When we are inwardly strong and spiritually fortified, big problems appear to us in the same light as little ones. If we knew as Jesus did that God is the power of our minds, and is working only for our good, then the seeming impossible, impregnable and incurable things would be shattered into a million bits.

This fact was brought out in a striking way by Jesus in His reply to the man who sought help for his "possessed" child, and because of its application here I am repeating the incident from my book, VITAL POINTS IN DEMONSTRATION.

"How long has he been like this?" asked Jesus.

"From a little child ... But if you possibly can, have compassion on us, and help us."

Jesus' amazement at this answer was shown plainly in His reply:

"WHY DO YOU SAY POSSIBLY?"

Why would you or anyone else ask such a ridiculous question? Don't you know that God is the one and only power in the Universe and that He is everywhere equally present? Don't you know that you partake of the Divine Nature? Don't you know that He is that nature? Don't you know the Law?

"Is anything hard for me? Is anything difficult?" "Why do you say possibly" to the One Power to whom nothing is impossible and Whose only purpose is to reveal and to fulfill Itself in every human need?

But listen to Jesus again. Let the "maniac son" represent your own big difficulty and you will see that He was talking to you as well as to the father of the afflicted child.

You have run the gamut of material means, doctors, serums, diets, psychiatry, healers, teachers, etc., and your difficulty remains unchanged. Everything else has failed and you now are back to the Source. You are back to the Great Physician, with renewed hope and determination but still asking the age-old question: "If you possibly can, will you help me?"

You still have a mixture of faith and unfaith, belief and unbelief. You reason that so many others have failed to heal your incompleteness that it hardly seems possible that even God can do it for you. You have unconsciously fallen into a failure complex, and each failure has caused your problem to seem larger than it really is.

But why should such a thing happen? Why should your prayers and petitions be so unavailing? St. Paul would say that you had been looking and praying to THE UNKNOWN GOD. "That which is born of the flesh is flesh, and that which is born of the Spirit is Spirit."

If you continue to identify yourself with the problem (personality), then you need never expect to identify yourself with its solution. Spirit and flesh are two and not one. One is truth and the other is a lie. One is power-full and the other is power-less.

How can you ever hope to be perfect until you identify yourself with that which is perfect? How can you ever hope to express freedom unless you identify yourself with that which is free? How can you ever hope to express health and. wealth without first identifying yourself with the Eternal Spirit which is ALL?

Jesus never identified himself with bondage, sickness, nor with things of the world. He showed the way out of bondage into freedom, out of sickness into health, out of poverty into wealth, and how to be in the world though not of it. He stated with emphasis: "No man cometh unto the Father but by ME." Not through any system, church, preacher, teacher, theory or form, but through the Self or "I" of all.

Who is Paul? Who is Matthew? Who is Mark? Who is Luke? Who is John? Who is Peter? Who is *me*? Verily, "I am God and Beside Me there is none else." "Thou shalt have no other Gods but ME." Is there any one or any thing besides Me? The answer is, "No. There is none else."

Then, who or what are you troubled about? What are you seeing? What are you hearing? What are you saying? What are you believing? Are you reacting to problems born of duality or are you considering your own consciousness? "What is that to thee; follow thou Me." Is there anyone or anything besides Me? Then why are you involved with, worried over, fearful for, troubled about any other? Don't you see how futile it is to be declaring the Presence and the absence of God all in the same breath?

If there is only One as Jesus said, then don't you see how foolish it is to try to set others right, and to straighten them out? Don't you see how puerile it is to declare the Presence and Power of God and at the same time to be seeing difficulties, problems, sin, sickness, ignorance and limitation?

Don't you see that it makes no difference how great or how small your problems may be? Don't you see that they must all be treated in the same way? Now answer me. Which is simpler and easier, to be struggling with persons, problems and things or to make the necessary corrections and adjustments in one's own consciousness? You know the answer without my telling you. Since Consciousness is the cause of whatever comes into our life and the cause of whatever leaves our life, then all adjustment and healing must take place in consciousness. It must take place by changing the image or belief we are holding.

Just as the artist transfers to canvas the landscape which he is beholding, so the troubled mind must get back to the Divine basis of the One. It must center itself in the ideal image or state of perfection it wishes to portray.

And how shall we proceed in such a matter? First, by taking all thought and feeling from the manifestation of evil, which we call Jack or Jill, problem or difficulty—by becoming absolutely "thoughtless" about it, by dissolving our belief in two powers. And, second, by finding a new master center and a new functioning of consciousness. In other words, by letting go and turning within as when Jesus said, "The Kingdom of God is within you." It is the unrecognized and unused portion of our own Self—the Real or Perfect Christ Man. Healing and demonstration do not come by changing conditions nor by adding anything to ourselves, but by revealing the power of our own minds.

If there is but One Self which is unconditioned, unlimited, unrestricted and free, then who is in difficulty? Who is conditioned? Who is limited? Who is restricted? Who is bound? Who is hopeless? Who is sick? Who is poor? There can be but one answer. No one, it is only a belief. And how can you prove this? By getting back to the Divine basis of the One, and by recognizing that you never have any concern or responsibility for anyone but yourself, that you follow no other than the One.

One day. One month. One year or twenty years. It makes no difference what the age, history or nature of your claim may be or whether you are looking for an answer or solution in the future. Jesus said that you must deal with it now. "Now is the accented time." "Now is the day of salvation." "You can never go into the past to make an adjustment—you must deal with your present thoughts of the past. And since w e can never live in the conditions we are approaching, called the future, we are compelled to also live the future right now."

But maybe you are puzzled about some decision you have to make and do not know which way to turn. Maybe you are seeking some bit of advice or the answer to some question. Maybe you are worried about the welfare or health of some loved one or friend. Then meet it now. Remind yourself that "I AM" is all there is of that one. "Beside me there is none else." "Hold fast that which is good." "If any man lack wisdom, let him ask of God, Who giveth to all men liberally, and upbraideth not."

Ask God. Ask your Real self the things you want to know and He will tell you. Trust God and depend on Him and "Do not," as Vivian May Williams says, "place any more reliance upon the advice of others than you do upon the judgment of your own mind, for what you actually do when you follow the advice of another is to act upon your own conception of his advice. We should rely upon the ideas, which come to our consciousness, more than we have been accustomed to doing, for Ideas are emanations from Divine Mind and they are the only means of communication with God. You really cannot boast of absolute dependence upon God until you learn to respect and rely upon the power of your own mind."

Then, how long, O Lord, is it going to take us to learn to do this? How long is it going to take us to learn to apply the simple principles contained in Jesus' lesson on "the lilies of the field" and the "fowls of the air?" Must we go on striving, straining, reaching, fearing forever?

Yes, I am talking to you, to myself and to the self of every person. This matter must be settled some time and it might as well be settled now. It will be settled when we "let go and let God." When we stop talking about failure to realize the truth, and the necessity of seeking the Truth, and realize that we are the Truth. Yes, my friend, you are that Glorious Self now, Omnipotent, Omniscient and Omnipresent.

Demonstration does not consist in turning sickness into health, limitation into plenty, confusion into peace and imperfection into perfection. It consists in realizing that health, plenty, peace and perfection are established facts which are automatically revealed when we cease to believe in sickness, limitation, confusion and imperfection. The quick way to spiritual demonstration then is through the realization that God is All there is in reality.

When Jesus was face to face with nebulous problems, insuperable difficulties and insurmountable tasks, He did not ask advice of others. "He stated the absolute Truth about God and man as they are in unity, oneness. His spiritual perception gave Him the necessary transparency of consciousness through which God and man could be seen in manifestation, . . . This is the only healing that can ever take place."

Let us remember, therefore, that no matter what the problem or difficulty we must never attack it directly, by headlong precipitancy or by pouncing upon it. Jesus said, "Consider the lilies . . . how they grow." Lilies do not attain their beauty by straining, worrying, fretting, but by indirection. They busy themselves in being what they are. They do not start out to get beauty by direct aggressiveness. It comes rather by virtue of what they are and by virtue of their willingness to be all that a lily can be. Their beauty is a consequence of absolute unity with earth air, sun and rain — of required conditions perfectly fulfilled.

How desperately we need to learn the lesson of the lilies! How desperately we need to learn to let go and to let God have our minds, our bodies, our souls, our hearts and our affairs! How desperately we need to turn from the many to the One, and to keep turning until our lives are re-polarized and power comes back again! That is why we need a new Master Center and a new functioning of consciousness. God's answers come not by tension, frontal attack or precipitate pursuit, but by understanding that we are God's Image and by imbibing His Truth. Corrections and adjustments come not by tinkering with problems nor by putting new patches on old garments, but by the inevitable out working of a new Ideal which has been made central in our minds.

If right now our lives fall into two parts, the larger part in the relative, or not self, and the smaller part in the Absolute, then let us heal this division and reverse this state of affairs by turning within to our Ideal of absolute victory over every human need. And what is this Ideal? It is the absolute conviction that God is all there is of everybody and everything. Let us concentrate every phase of our consciousness on this Ideal until it takes root in every last detail of our lives. Let us know that at the Center of our being is the Living God Who is not only equal to, but greater than, anything that can happen to us or that can come into our lives.

Let us know, as St. Paul said, that we can "do all things through Christ which strengtheneth us." Let us know that when the tyrannical clutch of the human mind has been dissolved and the Christ Mind acts independently of our own, God will have a fructifying consequence in our lives. We will not only have the power to alter circumstances and surmount obstacles; we will have the power to accomplish whatever needs to be done. Difficulties will no longer loom big or hard, for we will have the power to transmute them into blessings. Our spiritual resistance will always be high and our problems, like diseases, be unable to "take hold."

And whence comes this power? It is all a question of consciousness and the polarity of our faith. When our faith in God is stronger and greater than our faith in our problem, then the problem will be solved quickly.

But let us see this obstacle complex in another light. Let us turn to the thirteenth chanter of the book of Numbers. The children of Israel are on their way out of bondage in Egypt to the Promised Land. They are now at the approaches to the land of Canaan and Moses sends out spies to bring back not only a description of the country, but specimens of the fruits that grow there. His instructions are simple and to the point. The information he wants must be accurate and complete. What kind of people dwell in the land? Are they strong or weak, few or many? Do they live in tents or in strong-holds? Will they likely offer much opposition? Is there wood in the land? Is it good land or bad land, is it fat or lean?

The assignment was carried out with speed, and after forty days the spies returned and made their report to Moses and the people. Now, visualize that vast company as the spies stood before them making their report and you will catch something of the conflicting emotions, the enthusiasm and pessimism, that filled the air. On one side the report gave a glowing account of a land flowing with milk and honey – a land so rich and fertile that it took two men to carry one bunch of grapes that grew there. And then there was the account of menacing obstacles which the spies believed made impossible possession of the land.

"We found giants in the land," they said, "massive fellows much stronger than we." And then they added this discouraging note: "And we were in our own sight as grasshoppers, and so we were in their sight."

There are many valuable lessons in this story, none more important than the necessity of right mental attitudes and the proper use of the imagination in overcoming the giants in our path. Right attitudes unify and simplify life, while wrong attitudes divide and complicate it. Failure is never in our environment but always in our imagination. It is a perfect illustration of an obstacle complex and an inferiority complex working together.

The real problem which the Children of Israel faced was not the conflict between desire and frustration. It was not the giants in Caanan but their grasshopper thoughts about themselves. The occupation of the land would be decided finally, not by the size or number of giants in the land, but by the mental attitude and ability to stand up and meet them.

St. Paul gave us the secret of meeting big difficulties in his epistle to the Ephesians: "Wherefore take unto you the whole armor of God, that ye may be able to withstand in the evil day, and having done all, to stand." And what does it mean to "take unto you the whole armor of God?" It means to dissolve all beliefs in two powers and to see only ONE—God, the Good Omnipotent. When that happens nothing in our world will seem difficult.

But they said, "We. were in our own sight as grasshoppers, and so we were in their sight." What a calamity! Here were thousands of able-bodied men and women held in bondage by an imaginary belief and the more they resisted the giants in their thought the more they accentuated their belief in them.

Of course, there are giants in the land and never more than now, but a giant as the dictionary tells us is "an imaginary being of great size." Note the word *imaginary* and then you will understand why giants (big difficulties as well as little ones) must be met and dissolved in the mind before they can be met and dissolved on the land. Big difficulties are only little difficulties magnified many times by our own imperfect sense of mental inferiority. Take the imaginative element (sense of inadequacy) from the mind; then your big difficulties will assume their natural size.

It is not uncommon for students from time to time to ponder the question as to whether they are growing in their spiritual work or standing still. There is one sure measuring rod to determine this, and that is our reactions to evil. It is always this reaction that determines growth or lack of it. If we are meeting these reactions by indirection, through the Father within, impersonally and without fear or strain, then we are growing. If we are becoming tangled up in them, worrying and fussing about them, then we are standing still.

In other words, we are "precisely like a ship in mid-ocean with the sails down and the power shut off." We are getting nowhere. "If Christ be not risen, then is our preaching in vain." If we still recognize two powers instead of One, then our prayers and our practice will be of no avail.

The really tragic people in every generation are the middle-aged "stay-at-homes." These are the real prodigals in every age, not because of their profligacy, indulgence and spendthrift habits, but because of their smugness, neglect of others and the stuffiness of their living. They have stopped growing, stopped being themselves. The glamour and the glory of their lives have gone out. The aspirations, the enthusiasms and hones of youth have settled into compromises, passivity and boredom.

This state of mind is tragic, for trouble ands calamity stalks the footsteps of those who have retired from life. Such persons would resent the appelation of prodigal, but, nevertheless, they are wasting the divine substance of life.

It makes no difference whether it be man, dog, potato or flower; if left untended and to themselves, they decay. When a man ceases to grow, he begins to perish. When he ceases to persevere and loses interest, he retrogrades and that rapidly. When he loses his courage to face life, he is a weakling. When he neglects his body, it falls apart. When he neglects his mind, he becomes a non-entity. When he neglects his soul, he becomes Godless.

The fault with such people is that they have lost the vision of God's purpose for them. God made man with "possibilities of full and glorious living" and to fail to realize these possibilities and to take advantage of them is to fail both God and ourselves. Let us realize then, that there is no provision in the Divine Scheme for mental and spiritual retirement or retrogression. We were intended to utilize the substance of life; to expand our living and to persevere to the very end.

The reason why one problem ever seems more formidable than another is because we try to meet it with only part of our mind, and because we hold limited and defective pictures of ourselves. Jesus said: "Thou shalt love the Lord thy God with ALL thy heart, and with ALL thy soul, and with ALL thy strength and with ALL thy mind."

You must center your whole self in God — heart, soul, strength and mind. Why? It is the secret of all spiritual attainment. Thus centered you not only will succeed in your every undertaking, but you will by-pass, surmount and outmaneuver the last obstacle that stands in your path. You will not do this by frontal attack, or the flanking movements of the human mind, but by indirection (laborless activity). In other words, God will, as He has promised, perform it for you and that without any effort on your part.

However, this is not easy. As Jesus pointed out, absolute relationship with God is required. That means perfect unity between yourself and the Father. It makes no difference if you call this unity "Cause arid effect," "God and man," "Spirit or identity," "Mind and its idea," or "Father and son." All refer to the One, unvarying, changeless, ever-living, ever-active principle of Good and Its Idea, which co-exist.

Man, being the perfect image of God, expresses all that God is, not by absorption Into God but by assumption of the Fact. What do we mean by assumption of the Fact? We mean the realization that the God innermost in us and the Most High God are One, and that if man is made in the image of the Other then the two must be alike.

That may sound involved at first reading. But it means simply that one cannot have more power nor be greater than the other and at the same time be identical. Did not Jesus promise that we would do greater works than He, and was not one of the accusations made against Him that "He made Himself as God?" He made Himself not God but "as God." In other words, He demonstrated the perfect unity between God and man. He assumed His sonship and His actions showed that He considered it actual.

We have thought of ourselves as being something separate and apart from God. We have considered two beings instead of one thereby losing our sense of unity and failing to demonstrate the principle of Good. Jesus said: "I and the Father are One," meaning that He not only possessed all power but that He was all power. Thus, the fact to be realized in quick demonstration over evil is that God is not separate from ourselves but is the Omnipotent Power of Good resident in our minds.

It is what St. Paul meant when he said: "Let this Mind be in you, which was also in Christ Jesus." When you clearly understand that God and your own consciousness are one and the same thing, then you have "Let that Mind be in you, which was also in Christ Jesus." In other words, you have put your mind under the control of God, whence it becomes the Power of God.

Now, contrast this position of Jesus with the position of the orthodox church and you will see why orthodox Christians fail so completely to demonstrate the Presence and Power of God in their affairs.

It is the difference between dependence upon a highly developed Self, with adequate resources for every need, and dependence upon an arbitrary and unreliable power.

Or would what follows be better than the statement above?

It is the difference between dependence upon a power over us and a power within us.

In three-dimensional Christianity the major emphasis is placed upon sin, which is the result of ignorance, and repentance, which is the result of fear of future consequences.

Rational theology, on the other hand, says that sin is a mistake, a missing of the mark, and that it brings no punishment but an inevitable consequence. Rational theology teaches man to depend upon the Inner Power in overcoming the world, to make himself so strong, so impregnable, through unity with God that nothing in the world can pull him down. It teaches man not only to depend upon God, but to cooperate with God.

The purpose of Jesus' life and teaching was not to make helpless slaves or dependents of human beings. It was to fortify them inwardly that they become superior to any difficulty that entered their lives. It is all right to exhort men to forsake and overcome sin — if they have character equal to the task. But to do so is a psychological impossibility if character is lacking. The Real way to help man overcome sin is to insulate him against it — to build up such a strong consciousness of the Presence of God that there will be no room in it for evil.

Human difficulties in their relation to Truth are like fires in their relation to water. Little fires can be put out with buckets of water; while big fires require tons of water. No one doubts that water can quench fire, but for big fires we must have it in quantity, and it must be intelligently applied. The amount and apparatus must be suited to the needs. If the fire is big, buckets will not do, but their inadequacy does not prove that water as an element has failed.

Do you see the lesson? Do you see its application to the big difficulties, even the disasters in your life? It means that your failure to meet them was due, not to God's reluctance or unwillingness, but to the narrowness of your consciousness, the inadequacy of your faith. Your consciousness of your problem was greater than your consciousness of God's Presence. It means that the forms of metaphysics and a small consciousness will not meet the great difficulties m your life any more than a few buckets of water thrown upon a big fire will extinguish it.

Does that mean, then, that water failed? Certainly not. It means that there was not enough of it. Does it mean that God failed? No. It means rather that your consciousness and faith were not absolute.

The only reason any one ever fails in a given demonstration is because of the in adequacy of his faith. The faith that moves mountains must be an absolute faith. There must be no doubt or opposition in it. Then why be frustrated by feeble experimentations and a shallow faith? What we need at such a time is not lamentations, but to be strengthened With might by God's Spirit in the inner man." Our great demonstrations will come, not by possessing God in the conscious mind only, but by being possessed by Him in the soul.

Now, let us see how the story of the children of Israel ends. Two men armed with God's Spirit volunteered to go over and subdue Canaan. The children of Israel were very skeptical of the adventure. They were filled with misgivings as to their ability to carry it out. However, when the day came and the two men were ready to go in. Joshua called the people together and said: "Tomorrow will the Lord do wonders among you."

Here was a tense moment. Here was the turning point in their history. Their whole future depended upon the success or failure of these two men; everything depended upon their faith and prowess. Were the children to continue in slavery or be free?

Imagine the reactions of the children of Israel when the announcement of victory came. Imagine their surprise when they learned how this momentous problem bad been met. The story says that the "Amorites' (giants) hearts melted." They collapsed, fell apart, shrivelled to their real size. The giants become pygmies and the pygmies become giants. Two men, armed with God's Presence, had faced the giants, and the giants lost their power.

But, there is another type of giant which we must consider before we leave the story. The first giants we meet are those in the outside world; the others are those we create within ourselves. We are not talking about rugged mountains to be climbed, natural barriers to be levelled, disagreeable persons to be met or unfortunate circumstances to be overcome. We are talking about the things WE HAVE TO DO; the difficult tasks, great responsibilities, unusual demands which life is putting upon us. Yes, those things surrounded as they most often are, with an overpowering sense of fear, frustration. worry, useless anticipation, and wasted energy.

Maybe you have never considered your disagreeable and difficult tasks in this light. But the truth is that the more you think about them and dread them, the harder they appear and the less power and ability you have to meet them. The fact is, what wears most people out is not the tasks nor the conditions they must meet but the frequency with which they revolve them in their thoughts. Why is this? Because dread and anticipation waste more energy than is required to perform the actual task.

Sometimes a job looks so big to us that we fear to begin it; we are afraid that we are not equal to it, doubt our ability to see it through. And what is the reason? The power we waste in anticipation and dread weakens us to the point of impotence.

The real problem here is not the demands which life makes upon us, but the destructive habit of magnifying our tasks and minimizing our powers. The solution lies in a reversal of the process. Instead of belittling ourselves and ascribing power to outside forces, we must take the opposite course. We must drop our attention from the task at hand and place it upon the Unconditioned Power of God. Thus, to bring the quickest and best results in any undertaking, we must not only see ourselves as greater than the thing acted upon, but all dread, fear and procrastination must be eliminated from our mind. And how shall we do that? By realizing that "Greater is He that is in us than he that is in the world."

Remember, we are never called upon to do anything, or to face anything that is beyond our power. That which comes to us comes because our inner spirit invited it. "Like attracts like and like begets like." Nevertheless if we did not have the inner resources to meet difficulties, they would not come to us. The psychologist will tell you that it is never the difficulty that defeats you but the lack of confidence in yourself.

There is a Promised Land awaiting you. There is an answer to every problem, a solution to every difficulty, and a supply for every need. But we will never find the riches of God's Kingdom if we seek them with only part of our mind, part of our heart, part of our strength and part of our soul. We must center our whole selves in God (commit our whole beings to Him); then we will become so strong, our power become so great that we will master every situation — our whole outlook will be changed, all our conditions will be changed. Fear and a feeling of inferiority and incompetency will then go out of our lives.

Then we shall no longer dread the future or tremble in the presence of hard tasks. We shall no longer lie awake nights milling over problems but shall turn them, lock, stock and barrel, over to God.

> **"Behind me is Infinite Power;**
> **Before me is endless possibility;**
> **Around me is boundless opportunity;**
> **Within me is certain victory."**

"THY KINGDOM COME ON EARTH AS IT IS IN HEAVEN"

The Kingdom of God as Jesus taught us is always present. But it must be recognized, realized and lived in. To become a power in our lives, the Kingdom must permeate our thoughts, not as form as in the case of intellectual assent, but as a force in absolute faith. It must be the predominating force in everything we think and do. "The man in the library may be ignorant. but the library in the man means knowledge. The man in the air may be dead, but the air in the man means life. So man may be in God yet if the door of the soul is closed, God is not in the man."

The really vital thing in meeting big problems, then, is a better quality of faith. Faith must have longer roots. W e must not only accept Truth in our minds, but embody it constantly in our thoughts. We must stop expecting conditions to change until we have changed ourselves.

When Jesus prayed, "Thy Kingdom come on earth as it is in Heaven," He was asking that heaven and earth operate as one. The terms "heaven" and "earth" mean literally that which is invisible and that which is visible.

"That which you realize within, the 'invisible,' will be 'visibly' expressed in what is commonly called the earth." Hence the prayer, "Thy Kingdom [invisible ideas] come on earth [be visibly expressed] as it is in Heaven." The contrast here, of course, is that between the "Absolute or Spiritual" and the "relative and material."

Most people think of these two planes as separate and distinct from each other and from themselves in time and space. The truth is that they are separated only by man's thought and because of his failure to harmonize them. Thus, the real intent of this part of the prayer is that we so unify the two realms that they work together in our thought. This is done by turning to the One Source. And why is this important? Because the cause of all inharmony is the dual belief in two powers instead of one.

When we, individually and collectively, cease to believe in a "material world" and a "material man," then sickness, sin, poverty and death will disappear from the earth. Why? Because there no longer will be anything in the consciousness of man through which sickness, sin, poverty and death can operate.

Aristotle said that "the animal soul [carnal mind] being conscious of perishable things perishes with them." This means that when the sense of duality has been dissolved the negative things which it seems to create will perish with it.

St. Paul said, "Seek those things which are above where Christ is," and again, "Every good and every perfect gift cometh down from above, from the Father of Lights, in whom there is no variableness, neither shadow made by turning." To most people the word "above" as used here would imply a "below," but, again, this is just another way of differentiating between the Absolute and the Relative. Taken together "above'; and "below" have the same connotation as the word metaphysics. *Meta* means over or above and *physics* means forms or matter.

Thus a metaphysician is one who thinks and works on the plane of that which IS. He goes "behind the plane of ordinary earth life into the concept of the Eternal. The ordinary earth life (relative) may be explained as that which is three-dimensional, and in which there is the conception of things occurring in sequence, which we call time. The metaphysical conception is that of a four-dimensional world, in which time has no place.

"The only difference between the ordinary doctrines of religion and metaphysical doctrines is the wider concept and deeper apprehension of reality which the metaphysician employs. He does not deny, contradict or cast aside any of the regular forms of faith any more than the aviator violates the laws of gravity when he flies. He simply employs a higher law which lifts him above the earth plane.

"So the metaphysician, going behind the relative (earth life) into the concept of the Absolute, employs a higher law which lifts him above the material. Persistently looking inward, he discovers those things which are without time and without change. He discovers for the first time the meaning of St. Paul's statement: "Christ in you the hope of glory . . ." "The same yesterday, today and forever," and that this Christ and his I AM are one and the same thing, having no time or changing content.

"Circumstances and conditions in which I AM functions may change, but the I AM itself does not change. It is something that simply IS." The metaphysician does not approach God through the outer relative world, but through the Kingdom of God within him.

"We make then this proposition: The changing factor in you, that which you observe as altering from day to day, infancy, childhood, youth, adult manhood, middle life, old age, is not the real you. You will find your true self when you discover within you that which is not in time, which eternally is. You will be able to practice metaphysical healing and 'do the works' when you are able to think and work in this consciousness rather than in the other.

"Take any of the familiar Truth statement—this one, for instance: 'I am the Radiant, All Wise, All Loving, All Conquering Son of God; I Rule Supreme Over All the Affairs of Mind and Body.' On which plane do you make this affirmation? If you make it on the plane of the changing and temporal you are uttering nonsense and perhaps blasphemy too. Not in that concept of your being do you know the radiant, all-wise, all-loving, and all-conquering son of God, nor does any changing thing have control over your mind or body.

"The eternal has power over the temporal; it is on the eternal plane that your affirmation is true. You cannot accomplish anything by your affirmations if there is anything in you that says that they are not true. This is the meaning of the requirement of 'faith.' But without understanding you do not gain faith and full confidence in the truth of what you affirm.

"If you have never learned and never consciously realized that there is an eternal existence, an everlasting now, and that this is where you really are at the present moment, you cannot successfully make affirmations of Truth. You must know that what you affirm is so.

"But suppose you have difficulty about affirming Truth when evil is so patently a fact—when say a man is suffering from what is called an incurable disease. Can you look with your eyes, with your senses all alive to a tragedy, and expect to gain anything by denying what you perceive to be a fact? By no means. But suppose that you lift your consciousness to the plane of the eternal and spiritual—what do you see there? Well, temporally speaking, this patient has been well for the greater part of his life and now there appears to be a change. When you contemplate the patient as I AM and as existing in an everlasting now, how can you fit the disease concept into that which eternally is? In the temporal (relative) sphere it is sequential, but in your exalted consciousness there is no sequence. How then can disease be?"

Don't you see that in the Christ consciousness there really is no incurable disease? Be perfectly honest with yourself— whichever plane you are working on. Do not say or affirm what you do not believe. If while in the Christ consciousness you affirm that there is no incurable disease you are absolutely honest with yourself."[2]

In spiritual therapy we think of the Absolute as the realm of cause, the Self-Existent, unrelated which nothing can disturb or limit, and we think of the earth or relative as the realm of effects or that which follows cause. The region of the first is in the Christ, "I AM" or Superconscious Mind, while the region of the second is in the human or conscious mind. The first exists by Itself alone, unconditioned, timeless, changeless and eternal, while the second exists by virtue of its relation to things transient, temporal and sequential.

---

[2] *The Christ Idea.* by H. B. E. Unity Monthly.

It is not hard to see, therefore, that to change circumstances and control conditions (which exist only in the relative), we must employ a higher law and a higher power which transcends the relative. We must learn to think, work and pray through the Absolute or Christ Mind. Our real work, then, is not to abrogate material or spiritual laws, but to use both for a common end as when Jesus said: "To this end was I born and for this cause came I into the world, that I might bear witness unto the Truth."

"Our citizenship is in heaven," as St. Paul said, but it is not until the eternal is manifested in the temporal (heaven and earth unified) that we shall be in a place where trouble and problems have no power over us.

Obviously, then, the important thing in creative and corrective work and the quickest way to success is to take our desires and intentions out of the lower plane, where they are limited and conditioned, and put them on the Higher plane, where they are unlimited and unconditioned. As we said elsewhere there are three realms in the universe corresponding to the three functions of the mind. They are the physical or material (conscious mind), functioning in time and where there is trouble, sickness, disease and poverty; the Soul or psychic (subconscious mind), which is the connecting link between the Higher and the lower, and the Spiritual or Absolute (without time), Superconscious or Christ Mind, and between the relative and Absolute stands the thought and the spoken word. "By the action of these two—thought and the spoken word—is the invisible made visible."

Thus the ideal in victorious prayer is to think and work in the Absolute, where the Christ Mind can work independently of our own mind as when Jesus said, "Of mine own self I can do nothing: The Father within He doeth the works." Then and then only does "the Truth revealed on the Higher plane have the power to heal the apparent evils of the lower plane."

It is not easy to make this point clear on paper but we shall be helped in this direction if we will think of the relative as the visible, or effect; of the Absolute as the invisible, or Cause, and of the subconscious as the medium, or transformer, through which the invisible is made visible. "And the Word became flesh and dwelt among us." "These three while in a way distinct are so blended into one that it is difficult to know where one ends and the other begins. All created things have spirit, soul and body. All things that we desire are now in being in the spiritual or Absolute."

Thus to bring the Kingdom of God on earth (the Absolute into the relative) as Jesus prayed, we must begin by taking our thought entirely off the relative and by centering it in God. We must harmonize our mind with His Mind as did Jesus when He said, "I and the Father are one."

With these truths before you, you are now ready to consider the technique of working in the Absolute, but before you do so the author asks that you count back sixteen paragraphs from where you are and read again carefully the instructions already given. Read these sixteen paragraphs, study them and meditate upon them until you understand them thoroughly.

THINKING AND WORKING IN THE ABSOLUTE

As an example of how this transition is made from the lower plane to the Higher, from the relative to the Absolute we will take a desire or intention and show how it is passed from the conditioned into the realm of the Un-Conditioned. The only requirements which the New Testament makes for this more perfect way of working and praying are first, that we give the "I AM," or Christ in us, full possession of our minds, bringing them up to that point of unity where we can say with St. Paul, "It is no longer I that live but Christ liveth in me," and second, that we do everything in and through the name of Jesus Christ. "Whatsoever ye do in word or deed, do all in the name of the Lord Jesus, giving thanks unto God the Father." "Whatsoever ye ask in my name He will give it you." "The name of the Lord is a strong tower the righteous runneth into it and are safe."

Turning now to the dictionary, we find that the word *name* means nature or character. Thus to pray in and through the name of Jesus Christ would mean praying in and through the character, nature or consciousness of Christ. In other words, we would be praying in or through the Absolute where God acts in our behalf and things come into manifestation without any interference, inhibitions, precedent or limitations of the relative or human mind.

When Jesus said, "If ye abide in me and my words abide in you, ye shall ask what ye win and it shall be done unto you," He was talking about His Consciousness. It is the Christ, or I AM, Consciousness in which metaphysical principles become operative and not the consciousness which is still on the material plane.

You would therefore, perform this operation, first, by letting "that Mind be in you, which was also in Christ Jesus," – perceiving that "God, Good and your consciousness are one." Second, by beholding yourself as the perfect man here and now. Third, by recognizing that as God's man you express all that God is. And, fourth, by realizing that you not only have all power but that you actually are all power now.

But let us stop for a moment to consider why we do not now have the things for which we have asked or prayed. Jesus said to His disciples, "Hitherto have ye asked nothing in MY NAME; Ask and ye shall receive, that your joy may be made full." The only reason we do not have the things we desire is because we tolerate a wrong relationship or connection, with God. We have prayed through the wrong name. We have prayed through our own name (consciousness), which is always relative and unfavorable to the things we ask, instead of praying through His Name. The result? Delay, frustration and disappointment.

St. James said: "Let not that man think that he shall receive anything from the Lord." Why not? Because, working from the lower plane, we have not only limited and conditioned the prayer by holding it in bondage to the relative, but we have set up a subconscious resistance to counteract its good effects.

The proper way, therefore, to take our desires out of the realm of the limited and conditioned and put them in the realm of the Unconditioned, is to pray without the intervention of personality. Since the Absolute is reached only through oneness with God, then we must purify our minds and desires from all relation to precedent, personal tension and the limiting conditions which usually attach to them. In other words, we must act with God's Mind instead of our own. We must pray with a mind free of doubts, fear, false beliefs, denial, limitation; in fact, free of everything which would in any way deny, divide or inhibit the good which we seek.

The next step is to impress your desire with absolute credulity and expectation (free from any limitations which pertain to it) upon the mechanism of the subconscious mind. Why the subconscious mind? Because it is the connecting link between your mind and God, the Universal Mind. You must first see the object of your desire as free from any limitations of human thought, conflict, precedent, circumstance, time or condition of the relative plane. There is no time but now.

Therefore, all time limitations must be ruled out. This is called cutting the cords, or freeing the desire from the unfavorable circumstances which always surround an intention held on the relative plane. Jesus said: "Whatsoever ye loose on earth shall be loosed in heaven."

The third step is to take the desire which has been freed from the limitations of the personal thought and to drive it still more deeply (through affirmation and concentration) into the Creative forces of the subconscious mind which, in turn, will impress it upon the Universal Mind. St. Paul referred to this process as "enlarging the borders of your tent," (increasing your consciousness), and the process should be repeated with conviction, definiteness, firmness, acceptance, regularity and individuality at least three times a day.

It makes no difference what the surface evidence or lack of it may be, just keep on keeping on. "Faith takes hold of the substance of the things hoped for, and brings into evidence the things not seen." Desire is the mould which the formless substance is to take. Our faith is the hammer which pounds it into shape. Our persistency shapes the substance into visible forms. Persistence is the power which brings it into visible form.

The fourth step is to visualize the desire as in instant fulfillment—to see it as a present fact, finished and complete in the absolute, or invisible. "Now is the accepted time." "Now

135

is the day of salvation" (fulfillment). "All things whatsoever ye pray and ask for, believe that ye have received them (in the Spiritual or Invisible) and ye shall have them." Believe that what you are seeking is already here. Believe that it is present though unseen, and through the continuity of your faith it will speedily spring forth into visible, or material form.

If this method of thinking and working in the Absolute seems mysterious and vague, the author suggests that you read again Jesus' parable of the sower and the seeds, and also the account of Creation in the first book of the Bible, and associate yourself with the facts and principles which they bring out.

We begin as God began In creation by speaking out into the formless substance all about us with faith and declaring:

"Let there be so and so (whatever we want). Let It come forth into manifestation here and now. It does come forth by the power of my word. It is done; it is manliest," etc., etc.

Always the plan of Creation is the same. First, the desire or image of the thing wanted. Second, the affirmation or impression of the desire upon the subconscious (without any discordant, contrary or conflicting elements), and then the revelation, or pressing out, of the form in response to Divine Law.

Now, let us review this process in order that we may clarify it and fix it steadfastly in our minds.

1. Make your desire as clear and definite as you can. Keeping in mind that desire, free from intense personal emotions and other inhibitions (already mentioned), attracts to you the good. It then becomes an attracting, magnetic force.

2. In forming your word (affirmation or image) make it correspond to the desire and see it as finished and perfect now. Go into it in detail and make it as definite in your consciousness as you can. Also make sure that there is no counter force in your consciousness, such as doubt, fear, misgiving or incredulity. In other words, see to it that your desire is purified of all negative emotions and contrary beliefs.

3. Synchronize your image with the subconscious mind, which in turn will synchronize it with the Universal Mind. The object is to get the image out of the conscious (relative) mind into the subconscious, and from the subconscious into the Superconscious, or Absolute. This can be done only through impression, concentration, realization and repetition.

   It is wise to repeat this process as many times a day as you consistently can, never less than morning, noon and night. In repeating your affirmation, impress the image strongly upon the subconscious mind with faith, firmness and persistence, and keep doing this regardless of whether or not any results appear.

4. Let it go and let it grow. In other words, keep the human, or primary, personality still. Still all its misgivings, false beliefs, doubts and fears, and cling tenaciously to the "Christ only." This is done to create balance between activity and passivity, and to give the image a chance to organize substance around itself. It is important that the work be allowed to rest until the program calls for another repetition.

5. Do not take the subject back into personal thought again. There is a tendency among many students not familiar with the finer points in demonstration to try to hurry or force results by the imposition of the human

will. They are afraid to rest their project in the belief that God will stop working when they stop thinking and affirming. Nothing could be further from the truth, however, because it is in this space between repetitions (when we have let the desire go and forgotten about it) that the greatest creative work is done in the subconscious mind.

6. Guard your image with your will. When negative suggestions and contrary thoughts come to you from the race mind, do not allow them to take root in your consciousness. Quickly cut them off by the deliberate action of your mind and keep willing them out until they cease to bother you.

The great trouble with many of us struggling with insoluble problems and insuperable difficulties is, that we have, consciously or unconsciously, separated ourselves in some way from the Great Magnetic Center of the Universe, which Jesus called the Kingdom of His Own Good. We are not properly related to our Source and so are attracting and perpetuating the wrong things. When trouble comes we have nothing to hold us up—nothing to see us through. We are like water on a slate roof.

"A man has to be made of steel to endure nowadays," read a suicide note recently. No, my friend, you do not need to be made of steel, but you do need to change your attitude toward life. You need to change your relation to it. In fact, that is the only problem there is.

When the young Hebrew men were about to be cast into the fiery furnace, they said: "Our God whom we serve is able to deliver us from the burning fiery furnace; and He will deliver us out of thy hand, but if not, know ye that we will not serve thy gods nor worship before the golden image which thou hast cast up." Note the words "BUT IF NOT."

The appraisal of man's faith in God should be determined not by the answer to some particular prayer or favor granted, but by how it stands up in the things that are foiled. The test of a ship is not what it does at anchor but how it rides the storm. The test of of a soldier is not what he does on the parade ground but how he conducts himself under fire.

Has not God said, "My ways are not your ways" nor "My thoughts your thoughts"; and, again, "The wisdom of man is foolishness with God?" Maybe we ought to pray again the prayer of Jesus: "Not my will, but Thine be done." Isn't failure after all but a horizon, and a horizon but the limit of our sight (understanding). Maybe our little ambitions and desires are set aside many times to prepare us for greater things.

"The failure of the caterpillar is the birth of the butterfly; the passing of the bud is the coming of the rose; the death or destruction of the seed is the prelude to its resurrection."

FAILURE IS A TEACHER

Job said: "Though he slay me, yet will I trust Him." When we have faith in God for God's sake; when we trust God for God's sake; love God for God's sake, then we shall see that failure is nothing more than one of God's teachers. Like the apparatus in the gymnasium, it is for the purpose of strengthening our mental and spiritual muscles, a part of the curriculum which leads us to higher levels. We shall then see that the only failure we need fear is the failure of not thinking and living with God.

When our plans fail maybe it is because God has a larger purpose in our lives. Maybe our little prayer is set aside for the moment that a larger purpose can be fulfilled. Maybe we ought to ask God to tell us what to ask for. Instead of asking Him for the things we want, maybe we should ask Him what He wants us to have.

We talk glibly about Jesus' Saviorhood, but we forget many times that the world was saved because He was not saved — from the cross. What a tragedy it would have been had God answered that smaller prayer to save Him from the cross, or if Jesus' faith in that tragic hour had turned upon Divine Intervention and God's willingness to save Him from the cross? Don't you see that it is the unanswered prayer many times that brings the greater blessing, and that we cannot know at such times what is best for us until we have His. Mind and can evaluate things as He evaluates them?

Is it not better under the circumstances, and wiser far, to let Him have His way in us? Is not the greater glory the glory of going on in spite of shock, disappointment, frustration and delay? To persevere in the face of failure; to be steadfast in defeat; to forge ahead in the face of indifference — these are the marks of a dauntless faith. To keep calm when others are losing their heads; to keep confident when others are losing their faith; to be hopeful when the condition is hopeless; to work on when you have failed — these are the tests of faith.

There never can be any question about the Divine Response to our prayers but many times there is a question about the things we ask. Not having the purely spiritual viewpoint, we do not always ask for the right things, nor do we have the mental equivalents for the things we ask. It is right and proper to ask for things ("all things") as the Bible says, but there is also an art in knowing how to ask for the right thing at the right time.

In the case of sorrow, for instance; it would not be wise to ask God to remove the sorrow from our lives, but to give us the strength and understanding to conquer it. What we need at such a time is clear vision and to be drawn closer to God, so that we may be closer to those who are with Him.

In a world like ours failures are just about as certain as disappointments. Too many of us are unnecessarily disturbed by them. "All have sinned, and come short of the glory of God." We all muff our opportunities and fall short of our highest goals. Defeat is more common than success. Life always is complex until we learn how to make it simple. We simplify it by changing our attitude toward it. We transmute our failures by refusing to allow them to solidify in our minds.

As the old Spanish proverb says: "We cannot prevent sparrows from flying over our heads, but we can prevent them from building nests in our hair." Behind so much frustration is unwillingness to build another ship and send it out again. Behind so much mediocrity is limp thinking. Behind so much fruitless effort is lack of self-confidence, self-faith. Behind so much physical sag is lack of inner harmony. Behind so much discord is lack of peace. Behind so much misery and suffering is lack of God.

THE HUMAN TENDENCY

It is a purely human tendency to want to be spared trouble, to evade difficulty and to want to be shielded from exacting situations. It would be so much easier to escape them or to let somebody else handle them for us. That is our way but it leads to weakness. God's way is to enlarge our ability and consciousness to meet these difficulties — to make us so strong on the inside that nothing in the outer world. can possibly affect us or throw us off balance.

As children of the King it is right for us to be strong, but strength comes, not from dodging or evading difficulties, but by facing and overcoming them. It is never God who fails us but we who fail ourselves. We do it through our shallow beliefs, limited capacities and imperfect knowledge of the Principle we use.

E. Stanley Jones tells of a famous surgeon and his son who were operating, on a patient when the father slumped beside the operating table with heart failure. The son saw at a glance that nothing could be done for his father; so without a moment's interruption he took over, carrying on the operation to a successful conclusion. Then he did what he could for the dead.

That son was never so great as when, amid the interruption of death, he continued faithful service to the living. He had no time for fruitless grief. His best service to his father was to carry on where the father had left off.

You pray that a certain deal may be consummated or that a certain change in your affairs be made, and you hope that it will—"BUT IF NOT" you send your spiritual roots down a little deeper. You pray that a certain financial need may be met, and you trust that it will—"BUT IF NOT" you seek a larger consciousness of God's abundance. You pray that a loved one may be healed and you hope that he will—"BUT IF NOT" you lift the Christ a little higher and seek a greater awareness of His Presence. You pray that your son may be protected in battle an d returned home safe. "BUT IF NOT" you enlarge your faith and ask God to give you the strength to pick up and go on.

In other words, you trust God in all situations and difficulties, not because of a particular answer to prayer, but because He is the only abiding and unchanging Presence in your life.

We are tortured not so much by the things that happen to us as by our reactions to them, the play of our imaginations and the unfortunate habit of crossing our bridges before we come to them. The remedy is to return to the Divine Presence for that cleansing which takes away the sins of the world. "If we confess our sins. God is faithful and just to forgive our sins, and to cleanse us from all unrighteousness."

"God's Heaven is so constructed at its core that It pours Its gifts only into the lives of those who are in the Father's House and, by the same token. It takes away from those who are separated from it. "To him that hath, to him shall be given and he that hath not, from him shall be taken away even that which he hath."

CONFESSION

The reason St. James tells us to confess our sins, faults and mistakes is purely psychological. Confession has the same meaning and purpose as Jesus' command to seek first the Kingdom of God. What is the purpose? To balance our minds and put them in the best possible condition to receive from God. Our religions should do this for us but they don't. In fact, most of them succeed only in filling the mind with morbidity, fear and self-condemnation. This always happens when one is made to feel guilt, to feel sinful or ashamed.

The Bible assures us that if we confess our sins (give them over to God), He will not only forgive us, but remember them no more against us forever. How could it be otherwise? "God is of purer eyes than to behold iniquity, and canst not look on evil." God is pure Spirit. Thus the quickest way to lose our troubles and receive healing is to get those troubles out of our subjective mind, to bare our souls to His Great White Light. It is not only one of the most practical methods of erasing our mistakes, but of letting go of trouble.

Sin means missing the mark, and while we continue to miss the mark we shall continue to perpetuate our suffering and pain. We should therefore enter the Presence every evening for a complete washing away of all the sins, worries, fears, mistakes and troubles of the day. "Behold the Lamb of God, which taketh away the sins of the world."

"Life can be organized around but one center." That center will be either the personal self or God. "Ye cannot serve God and mammon." No wonder Jesus told the rich young man to go sell all that he had and "come follow me." No wonder that He tells you to return to the Father's House, where there is bread enough and to spare, "to seek first His Kingdom and His righteousness." Healing is there. Power is there. Peace is there. Economic security is there. Happiness is there. Comfort is there. Success is there. All await your recognition and appropriation.

Are you tired of eating husks of trouble and difficulty? Are you tired of living in the pigsty of failure, blocked passageways, disappointments, defeats and delays? Then follow the advice of Jesus: "Seek ye first His Kingdom and His righteousness, and all these things shall be added unto you" — and from Job: "If you return to the Almighty, thou shalt be built up, thou shalt put away iniquity (trouble) far from thy tabernacles."

Maeterlinck once said: "In owning our faults we disown them; and in confessing our sins they cease to be ours. Thus by confession Christ sets us free."

PUT THE KINGDOM OF GOD FIRST

Did you ever wonder why it was that Jesus told you to put the Kingdom of God first? It was because the Kingdom is the Source of everything, and being the Source of everything has the power, (when you are properly related to It), to produce everything you need or desire. That is why He told you to put the Kingdom first — because everything you require will be added when your first thought is given to His Presence. "Seek ye first His Kingdom" means literally to go to Him first in every need, to trust Him for everything and to live so close to His presence that you are conscious of Heaven at every moment.

To seek His Righteousness is to live in harmony with God's Law and to hold the right attitude toward all persons, problems, conditions and things. Righteous action is harmonious action, and harmonious action works for the highest and the best at all times.

To enter God's Kingdom is to change your life and to enlarge your consciousness — to enter into more health and power; and the more power you grow into, the more you will give to the body and the mind. To enter into the Kingdom is to grow out of all bondage; one problem after another will disappear until you are absolutely free. By seeking the Kingdom first, you receive everything that is required to make your life full and complete. "You receive everything you want from the within, and you gain the power to produce everything you want in the with out" — not just a few things, but all things.

Thus the high meaning of seeking the Kingdom first is to look to God and to place your greatest dependence upon His Power for all things at all times. In other words, you are to look to God and receive from God and not man.

In the largest sense God's Kingdom comprises the entire universe, but for you and for me it simply is a matter of our consciousness of His Presence. Your Kingdom and my Kingdom simply is the measure of our faith in God how much we trust Him in our needs and how much dependence we place upon Him in our thoughts. Our experience of it is determined by our attitude toward life, and by what we are most intimately and vitally attuned to. It is determined by our conviction of God's instant and unfailing help regardless of what may be happening in our affairs. It is determined by our faith in the triumph of righteousness even when everything about us may seem to be falling apart.

Jesus said: "It is your Father's good pleasure to give you the Kingdom." But before you can receive the Kingdom you must have a mental equivalent, or affinity, for it. You must be "born anew" into the consciousness of His Ever-Presence. You must individually conceive and emphasize the concept in practice that "There is only One Presence and One Power in the universe, and It is all Good and All Powerful."

IS THIS TRUE IN YOUR CASE?

But is this true in your case? When things go bad with you, or with some loved one; when you are sick or some loved one is in difficulty; when your bills are overdue and you cannot meet your obligations; when you are frightened, frustrated and sad, then do you give in to these enemies? Do you believe that any one or all of them combined are more powerful than your God? If you do, then you have taken yourself out of His Kingdom and placed yourself under the curse of the Law. In your own mind you have weakened the very power that was able to deliver you.

Did God, then, fail? No, you failed God. You failed Him by giving more power to outer ills than to inner realities. You failed Him by giving more power to the material than to the spiritual.

Now, answer these questions for yourself: Can a stream rise higher than its Source? Can you rise higher than your faith in God, higher than your faith in yourself? Can you win success in anything unless you expect it, demand it, and accent it? Isn't it clear to you that you can rise above a lesser power only by employing a greater power, and that a great success must have a great source in consciousness, in realization, in faith and in untiring effort to attain it?

Don't you see that the result can never be larger than its cause, and that your achievement can never rise higher than your faith? Then where are you falling down? I'll tell you where. You have not aroused the sleeping giant within yourself. You are trying to run your life with one cylinder instead of eight. You have the power but are not using it. You are like the moon, trying to shine by reflected light.

It doesn't matter how uncongenial your environment may be, nor how many problems you may have, there is just one force by which you can change them—the Spirit of the Consciousness of the Presence of God. The statue will always follow the model, and the model is your consciousness of the Kingdom within you.

The great curse of the people who are failing to get anywhere is apathy and lethargy. They have the power but won't develop it and use it. They go just so far and then stop. Or maybe they "pass the buck" to somebody else. What is the result? They lose the power they have. Instead of commanding the forces about them, they are commanded by them. Instead of pushing, they are being pushed.

Perhaps it was this weakness which Jesus had in mind when He said that the Kingdom of Heaven is taken by violence. Those who would attain it must assert themselves. Otherwise they will go down hill and not up.

"If we choose to be no more than clods of clay," said Marie Corelli, "then we shall be used as clods of clay for braver feet to trod on." If your mind is divided or your consciousness is turned downward in favor of evil; if you lack self-confidence; if your faith in God is no bigger than your faith in your problem; if you doubt your ability to get what you go after, to accomplish what you set out to do; if you fear to make a change when it is necessary, or fear that others are more capable than you; if the negatives preponderate in your mind, then you cannot hope to change your circumstances. No, not until your whole consciousness has been changed, or until you have established an unfaltering faith both in God and in yourself.

Power originates in a fully surrendered mind and runs parallel with the aim. It cannot achieve great things when it is diluted with little thoughts. A prayer feebly born will be feebly expressed. Unless there is vigor of conception, there will be indifferent execution.

ACCORDING TO YOUR FAITH

"According to your faith," said Jesus, "be it done unto you." Not according to the faith of your priest, minister, or of some member of your family, but according to YOUR faith—YOUR faith in God, YOUR faith in yourself, YOUR faith in your goal, YOUR faith in your ability. The man of little faith gets small results, while the man of big faith gets great results.

Just as it is the intensity of the heat that melts the iron ore and makes it possible to mold it into shape, so it is the fixity of vision and invincibility of purpose which carries a man successfully to his goal. "According to your faith" means literally according to your acceptance of God. To be in tune with the Infinite is to be in touch with your Source.

When your trolley is on the wire, you will be in constant touch with your good. If your trolley slips off the wire, if you constantly are losing the connection (by negative thoughts), you will be impotent, powerless. And how can you keep your trolley on the wire and maintain connection with the power, how bring the power into expression? By keeping your thoughts upon God.

The reason Jesus laid so much stress on faith was because it is the only attitude that can keep a man in touch with the Divine Current. Self-faith is like a charged magnet. It will multiply the individual's power as nothing else can do. It will make a one-talent man a power, while a ten-talent man without it will be weak. Jesus illustrated all this in His lesson on the vine and the branches. "I am the Vine, ye are the branches." When a man is in contact with God, he receives the power of God. He then is in touch with all that is whole, perfect and true. When he is out of touch with God, he is like a flower broken from its stem. Separated from the Source of Life, he begins to wither and fade.

How then shall we stop this disintegrating process? By getting a fresh connection with God. "If thou return to the Almighty, thou shalt be built up." If there is a sense of Inferiority in you, then it is because you have put it there. If you had the understanding of the Kingdom of God within you and lived in it, then you would be superior. You thought yourself into this condition of inferiority, and when you think with God (upwards), you will think yourself out of it.

But what are these conditions which try your soul? What are these problems which baffle you, these doubts that darken your vision, these fears that paralyze your efforts; what are these ghosts that haunt you, who are these people who offer you so much opposition? They are nothing but your own thoughts about the things that are happening to you. They have power only because you are away from the Father's House, because you are thinking about self and without God.

How then can you change the gravity of adverse circumstances and cause them to serve you? By entering God's Kingdom. When you give yourself and all your affairs into the Father's hands, when you give your whole consciousness to Him, then all negative suggestions, all negative circumstances will lose their power over you. Then there will no longer be anything to fear, because God has given you the "power of a sound mind."

BLESS YOUR CIRCUMSTANCES

"Not by might, nor by power, but by my Spirit, saith the Lord of Hosts." When your thought is lifted to God, His love flows into you in a mighty, cleansing tide. You now can bless your circumstances and put to flight all that is adverse by calling out the good that is in them. To the fear that has caused you anxiety you can say: "I bless you with God's peace and harmony." To the person who has injured and opposed you: "For the good that is in you, I bless you and bless you." To the obligation that is in default: "I bless you with God's abundance and prosperity." To the sick person: "I bless you with God's wholeness and perfection."

In the consciousness of God's Presence you can bless every adverse circumstance right out of existence, not by the feeble energy of the human mind, but by the quickening Power of the Mighty Christ within you." "By my Spirit, saith the Lord of Hosts." And what you loose in heaven (mind) is loosed on earth.

In speaking of the Kingdom of God, Jesus left nothing to the imagination. He told us where it was, when it was and how to find it. "Neither shall they say, Lo, here! or, Lo, there! for, behold, the Kingdom of God is within you." "The Kingdom of God is at hand." "Seek, and ye shall find; knock, and it shall be opened unto you." "Except one be born anew, he cannot see the Kingdom of God." "It is your Father's good pleasure to give you Kingdom." "I speak not from myself: but the Father abiding in me doeth His works." "These things have I spoken unto you that my joy may be in you, and that your joy may be made full."

From His Kingdom proceeds everything necessary for successful and bountiful living, health, supply, strength, peace, power and wisdom; and in it there is nothing unlike God — no fear, no worry, no frustration, no loss, no inferiority, no doubt, no disease, no weakness, no poverty, no discord and no failure. Nothing of a negative character can possibly stand against the power of Almighty God. "And this is the work of God, that ye believe." Believe what? Believe in God with all your heart. Believe in God with all your soul. Believe in God with all your mind. Believe in yourself with all your might.

COOPERATING WITH THE KINGDOM

When you pray THY KINGDOM COME you must believe, as St. Paul says, that all things are possible through Christ. Through your consciousness of His Presence and your faith in His Power, your problems can be solved, your difficulties can be met, your desires can be fulfilled, your deficiencies can be overcome, your sickness can be healed, your differences can be adjusted, separations can be united, and "death can end in resurrection." Truth students everywhere have proved these things, and so can you.

Second, you must know that when you work in the Kingdom consciousness you are using spiritual laws instead of natural laws, and that the spiritual is not contrary to the natural but transcends it. The higher law always takes precedence over the lower. The power that answers prayer, cures the incurable, makes possible the impossible and gives courage to the weak merely transcends the law of the physical. "If ye be in Christ Jesus," said St. Paul, "ye are above the law (of the physical) and not subject to it."

In other words, human ills and difficulties lose their power to hurt in the presence of the Greater power which heals. Just as a condemned man is suddenly saved by the higher law of the Governor who reprieves him, and heavier-than-air machines are made to fly by a higher law than the physical, so the God-centered man rises above his difficulties through the stronger law resident in his mind.

Then, third, you must cooperate with the Laws of the Kingdom. (You will find them listed in the Sermon on The Mount, in the fifth and sixth chapters of St. Matthew's Gospel.) This means that you must live, think and act in the positive, affirmative and constructive side of food, and that you must keep yourself in harmony with the Principle of Good at all times. It means that you must keep the stream of consciousness pure by protecting it at its source, by keeping out of your mind all the thought poisons, the petty annoyances, irritating suggestions, inhibitions and depressions, and by refusing ever to think of anything you do not want manifested in your life.

To cooperate with God you must continually see yourself as you are in Him — free, whole, perfect and complete. There is no entrance fee to God's Kingdom but your willingness to do His Will. There is no requirement but to have His Mind.

The laws of the Kingdom are all summed up in the great law, "Thou shalt love the Lord Thy God with all thy heart, and with all thy soul, and with all thy mind, and thou shalt love thy neighbor as thyself." Regardless of how difficult this law may be, it is the secret of all successful achievement. It will bring angels down to earth and lift men up to Heaven. It will transcend every physical law known. It will abrogate weakness and expand power. It will do everything you want done and undo everything you want undone.

Yes, the Kingdom of Heaven will come through love, and it cannot come in any other way. When you let God into your life His Love will radiate from your heart. His light will shine from your mind. His Power will work for you and His Peace will be in you.

Are you ready to enter God's Kingdom and live under Its rule? Then you can do so in proportionate degree as you recognize It and give your consciousness to It; as you put off self and remove all negatives from your mind; as you ignore all appearances and recreate all affirmatives; as you live and think in the present and control your thoughts so that nothing poisonous creeps in.

The Kingdom of God is not a physical place like a town or city, but a state of mind. In its unrecognized state it might be said to be very much like the little rubber toys in the shape of cats, dogs, elephants, roosters, etc. As you look at these miniature rubber bags lying on the counter, they are quite shapeless and unattractive. But when they are blown up, they immediately assume the definite shapes of the animals and fowls they are intended to portray. The elephant was there all the time, but he was not discernible until the bag was filled with air.

And so it is with the Kingdom of God. Until it is recognized and embodied in our thought, it is just as though it did not exist. It is just a possibility. How then shall we "blow up" this Idea and give It form? By contemplation of the Spirit, and by raising our thoughts to God.

The Kingdom of Heaven will grow up in you as you grow up in God. It will develop and expand and fill your life exactly to the degree that you keep your thought pure. It will take definite shape as a new creature new ability and new power just to the degree that you give it first place in your life. As you keep your mind on Heaven It will grow by Itself, automatically, like the mustard seed or the yeast in the lump of dough.

Your Heaven will be your consciousness of It. It will be made up of your consciousness of God's Presence, your awareness of His instant and unfailing help, your unfaltering faith in His unlimited Power, your reliance upon His Judgment, your obedience to His Law, your willingness to be guided by His Wisdom, your determination to have His Mind, your surrender to His Will. IN THESE, LIES YOUR OWN "KINGDOM OF GOD," TO WHICH "ALL THESE THINGS" SHALL BE ADDED.

It is right for you to want things, to ask for things and to have them, but you must put first things first. "Seek ye first the Kingdom of God and His righteousness, and all these things shall be added unto you." Put God first and your needs shall be met. Put your needs first and your needs will increase. That is the law; and until you conform to it, you will get no good results from your work.

The things that are easy of attainment when your mind is filled with God are almost unobtainable when your mind is filled with self. If you put your sickness first, it will not be healed. If you put your debt first, it will not be paid. If you put your problem first, it will not be solved. "Ye seek me for the loaves and fishes; and cannot find me."

If you put anything before God, you will fail. The law states clearly, "Thou shalt have no other gods before me." You shall not give power to difficulties, discords, inharmonies, appearances or inadequacies. "I am God and beside me there is none else." The prior condition therefore to getting what you want is to put God first in every need. If you fail in this, then you break the circuits and keep yourself in a state of separation.

YOU CANNOT CHANGE GOD

It is a satisfying feeling that comes with the knowledge that you cannot change God with prayers, thoughts and words; that you cannot change Him by concentration willing, or by trying to compel things to happen. God does not work that way, and the sooner we discover this fact the better. Jesus said, "What things soever ye desire, when ye pray, believe that ye have received them." Receiving from God is merely providing an outlet for His Good. In metaphysics we call this outlet a mental equivalent (belief) through which God may express Himself In terms of His own Nature. You do not concentrate or will that electricity light your house; you provide ways for it to light your house.

When Jesus told his disciples to "seek first the Kingdom of God." He really was telling them to harmonize their minds with God's Mind, to put their minds in the best possible condition to attract from His Kingdom everything they needed. Would you put yourself on the receiving end of the Law? Then put God first, and you will definitely make a magnet of your mind which, by an inevitable principle of attraction, will bring to you everything God intends you to have.

All things needful will then flow to you in abundant measure. You will then have the power not only to attract everything you need, but to get rid of most things that you do not want.

And it all hinges upon a perfect relationship between your mind and His Mind:

"No negative thought form can come between me and my realization of God's presence in every part of my being."

"I am increasing mightily in the power to express Divine Goodness."

Robert A. Russell

Raisa - Mystic Alchemist

Energy Healing, Chakra Alignment, Sacred Geometry, Sound Healing

Tammy:
I was blessed with a healing session by Raisa last week. She felt like a friend and like-minded gentle soul with comforting Mother Mary essence pouring through her words. Raisa was so in-tuned to my blocks and traumas held within my field. She used her connection to ascended masters I've resonated with such as Yeshua, Mother Mary, Mary Magdalene, Lady Vesta & Amethyst and archangels Metatron, Michael and others to help clear these.

I was able to address childhood trauma situations to flip the stuck energy I've held onto over the years. She also picked up on a few traumatic past-life scenes that have affected my current life. I am an intuitive energy healer who truly felt the shift and healing within. I now feel so much lighter and have clarity regarding my path.

So much love and gratitude to you both, Raisa and Barry for presenting her to my world! (More Testimonials on following Pages)

Contact Raisa to book an Energy Healing
or Chakra Alignment session:
www.RaisinYourIsness.com
raisinyourisness@hotmail.com

Shannon:

This BEAUTIFUL sister...our Raisa... is a treasure beyond compare! After my experience in my personal session with Raisa... the ABSOLUTE confirmation I received, that could ONLY be confirmed by HER mind you... this session solidified EVERYTHING for me. I KNOW that this sister... she is a formidable, magnificent & IRREPLACEABLE component in this Earth plane story we all are invested in! IF YOU ARE DRAWN TO HER FOLLOW YOUR HEART

No other can do what SHE is gifted to do for YOU... YES YOU!

I LOVE YOU dear sister! I am forever grateful for what only you could do and DID for me! I would have happily paid any price for what you gave me! I URGE YOU ALL to schedule a session with this beloved one!

P.S. thank you Barry for sharing her with us all!

∞

Natasha:

I would like to thank Barry for introducing us to Raisa. I have had 2 consultations with her in the last month and I am in total awe of what transpired. Raisa is such a beautiful caring soul! She connected with me as though she has known me forever. Her love and dedication in assisting others is so touching. I had an amazing experience and some profound healing. I received a message from Jeshua which brought tears to my eyes. I could feel the LOVE in the message that was given to me and I will remember and cherish His message forever. Raisa has really helped me in confronting fears, trauma and past life karma. I have found the reason for my skin problems which I never would have thought it'd be possible. It is amazing what guilt and shame from past lives can actually do to your body. Her healing and that from our Angelic beings has really made a huge difference in my life. I can feel it in my energy. Raisa has a lovely sense of humour, always reminding you not to take life and yourself so seriously. I really feel like a heavy weight has been lifted off my soul. Thank you so much! Much Love!

∞

Ariel:

Raisa... Divine Raisa... You are a Treasure to this Life, and I thank All That Is, and this also Treasured YT channel for the priceless blessing which was our session this AM. Every moment of the session was a fractal explosion of wonderful intuitive & divinely guided perfection. I honor your sincere, caring, graceful, playful, soothing, encouraging, transformational, empowering, and so beautiful demonstration / embodiment of Goddess energy and presence. I am so honored & thankful to have been guided to You. To have invested in the patience, time, energy, and resources to share sacred healing and uplifting time with You. I will remember the session Always. And I will look forward to any and all ways our Creator deems it harmonious to connect again. I could go on and on and on, so please accept my parting acknowledgment of your blessing to this realm, my Heart & Spirt, my Life, and the Lives of all those who may be positively impacted via your assistance. Blessings, and Gratitude, a thousand times over and over again. Namaste... Namaste... Namaste...

∞

B.G.

I have just finished a healing session with Raisa. The experience was remarkable! I am still buzzing! I heard about her from this channel, so thank you deeply Barry!

Raisa is so lovely to talk to, and intuitively guided, knows how to get to the hidden roots of our issues. She calls upon ascended masters, archangels and such to do deep energetic clearing and healing work. It was like being guided through the deep layers of myself, releasing the things that don't serve me and filling every cell with light. I purged, and I absorbed new energy, and came out feeling uplifted and renewed. Raisa helped me to find things in myself that I had been cut off from, and to heal wounds I had tried to bury. She has also given me helpful ideas to continue to improve things my life.

I am so blessed to have found Raisa, and ever grateful for the healing work she has done. She is as authentic as they come. Truly an earth angel! Thank you, thank you, thank you!

▶ YouTube

YouTube Channels of Interest:

Giving Voice to the Wisdom of the Ages

Over 5,000 audios, hundreds of
Spiritual and Metaphysical
audio books including
Robert A Russell, Dr Murdo MacDonald Bayne,
Napoleon Hill, Jeshua, Kryon and many more.

I AM Meditations and Affirmations

Hundreds of I AM Meditations,
Daily affirmations and more.

Raisin' Your Isness

Metaphysical Musings, Channelings,
Sound Healing Songs

www.ingramcontent.com/pod-product-compliance
Lightning Source LLC
Chambersburg PA
CBHW031301090426
42742CB00007B/557